MW00634650

Connecting with Your Ancestors

Connecting with Your Ancestors:

A Practical Guide for Living a Destiny-Driven Life

Dr. Asanee Brogan

Copyright © 2021 Asanee 44 LLC
All rights reserved.
ISBN: 978-1-7379170-0-7

About the Author

Dr. Asanee Brogan is an experienced life coach, consultant, writer, and professor. She has worked and lived in many regions throughout the world, inclusive of West Africa, the Middle East, Europe, Southeast Asia, and the Caribbean Islands. Dr. Asanee serves as the Principal Coach and CEO of Asanee Coaching Services and is a partner of the Ginen platform. She and her staff offer a variety of services through this organization, inclusive of spiritual, business, career, and financial coaching.

As a practitioner of two African spiritual systems, Asanee also creates and publishes spiritual coaching tools. She is a devotee of both the Ifa and Haitian vodou spiritual systems. Her experience in both of these systems has been instrumental in the development of her knowledge and understanding of spiritism as a whole. She makes a humble attempt of relaying her ever-growing knowledge of this subject through coaching, writing, teaching, and mentoring.

Table of Contents

Introduction

If you are reading this book, your ancestors have already made contact with you. In fact, ancestral spirits continually make contact with each of us every day. However, not everyone is aware of this contact. As such, some people do not seek to understand or reciprocate communication with their ancestors.

Many people who were raised in westernized societies and indoctrinated in Abrahamic religious systems do not actively participate in ancestor *veneration*. They aren't aware of what ancestor veneration is or how to actively engage in the process. Instead, many people fear this practice because they equate it to devil worship or some other form of Satanism.

However, ancestor veneration is the act of consciously and intentionally honoring our lost loved ones. This practice is often referred to as ancestor worship in the western world. Sadly, due to colonization, ancestor veneration has been demonized to a great extent. Using the phrase "ancestor worship" is part of this demonization process. According to Abrahamic religious systems, worship is solely reserved for one sovereign god or deity.

In which case, worshiping or venerating any other spirit or deity is deemed evil and sinful. Adherents of such religions assume that those who engage in ancestral veneration are worshiping their ancestors. In reality, individuals who engage in this practice are simply paying homage to the good and benevolent spirits who are part of their bloodline.

This form of honor or reverence tends to lead to a stronger bond with their lost and *living* loved ones. In fact, it can lead to a better overall life for those who consistently engage in this practice. Depending on the depth of one's practice, it may even open doors of opportunity for future generations.

So, if your ancestors have been tapping on your door, don't be afraid to open it. You can do so with confidence knowing that you are opening up a door of blessings for you and your family. As you develop a safe and responsible practice, you can tap into the bountiful resources that your ancestors are waiting to offer you.

Chapter 1: Who are Your Ancestors?

According to the commonly accepted westernized definition, ancestors are individuals from whom we are descended. Thus, your ancestors technically include both living and dead individuals from your lineage according to this definition. And, there is no distinction made regarding the character of these individuals.

Contrarily, in traditional belief systems of Africa, Asia, the Caribbean, and other parts of the world, our ancestors are defined as a specific group of deceased loved ones. In these traditions, ancestors are lost loved ones who have transitioned to the ancestral realm. The ancestral realm is a sacred gateway reserved for individuals who lived good and benevolent lives while on earth. They epitomized strong moral character and ethical values that allowed them to ascend to a higher level in the astral or heavenly realm. Most often, these individuals contributed to the betterment or advancement of their families, communities, or society at large in some way.

Therefore, according to traditional belief systems, not all of our deceased loved ones are ancestors. Only those who lived a life of sound character are included in this group. Therefore, when I speak of ancestors throughout this book, I am specifically referring to those individuals who positively contributed to the growth and advancement of their family line, the community, or society at large.

3

Also, ancestors are inclusive of individuals from both sides of an individual's family line. We all have ancestors from both of our biological paternal and maternal lineage. This is irrespective of whether we knew these individuals or not. Additionally, we have many ancestors who passed away decades or centuries before we were born, meaning we have many ancestors that we do not know about.

It is important to keep this in mind because any of your ancestors may be walking with you at any given moment. Though you may have had a close connection with your ancestors from one side of your family, your ancestors from the other side of your family may be assisting you. For instance, you may have grown up around your mom's family and have a close-knit relationship with them. However, you may not know your dad or anyone from his family line. But, most of the ancestral spirits that work with you could be from your dad's side of the family. Therefore, as you venture into the practice of ancestor veneration, keep in mind that we don't get to choose the spirits that work with us - they choose us.

So be careful about being ungrateful or indignant regarding the ancestors who are walking with you. Even if you disliked specific individuals when they were living, these same individuals might be assigned to guide and protect you once they pass to the ancestor realm. Instead, consider it a blessing that you have

4

lost loved ones who are willing and able to help you regardless of who they are.

There are tools that you can and should use to reconcile broken relationships. However, don't neglect your ancestors due to disdain or hate. Doing so will only hinder or delay your ability to fulfill your destiny because that is the ultimate goal of ancestor veneration.

Chapter 2: Why Connect with Your Ancestors?

Many people don't understand ancestor veneration because of the mechanisms involved in this practice. From an outsider's perspective, ancestor veneration may appear to be a foolish or unfruitful endeavor. However, the rituals performed for the purpose of honoring our ancestors actually serve a profound purpose. Once you understand the mechanisms and meaning of the process, you can begin enjoying a more effective and productive life.

Though, it must be iterated that honoring your ancestors will not make your life perfect. Your ancestors will not remove every obstacle or challenge that you face. Instead, they may make the road easier and your burdens lighter. They can also direct you to the proper tools and resources so that your journey is successful and less taxing. Contrarily, they may put specific roadblocks in your way to prevent you from going down the wrong path. So don't dismiss all challenges or obstacles as evil or malicious because your ancestors may just be using them to save your life.

An analogy of how our ancestors work in our lives is taking a journey in the desert heat. You can choose to walk, or you can choose to drive. If you decide to walk, it could take more than 7 hours to reach your destination. However, it could take about 30 minutes to get to the same place if you use a vehicle. Obviously, if you walk, you will endure more challenges and hardships than if you drive. If you are taking the journey during extreme heat conditions, you will definitely experience greater challenges. You will have to take many pitstops for water, rest, food, etc. It will be necessary to avoid getting hit by oncoming vehicles, and you will possibly have to be on guard for wild animals. Of course, you will be sweaty, thirsty, and exhausted by the time you get to your destination. Even more, depending on the time you set out on your journey, it may be dark by the time you get there.

On the other hand, if you drive, you can avoid many obstacles and delays that are common during a journey by foot. Obviously, you must be awake and alert to properly maneuver your automobile. And, you will still have to look out for other vehicles, flying rocks, gravel, objects on the road, potholes, etc. To avoid an accident, you will also have to be wary of adverse weather conditions such as strong winds, rain storms, etc.

However, your journey will be much smoother when driving in a well-operating vehicle. You will have access to air conditioning to keep you cool and comfortable. You can even listen to music or enjoy another source of entertainment to keep you company along the way. Also, you don't have to worry about the threat of losing battery power on your phone when traveling by vehicle as you would if you were walking. Ultimately, you will get to your destination much faster and with less stress and exhaustion if you drive rather than walk.

This is the difference between walking life's journey alone versus with our ancestors. Our ancestors are like the vehicle mentioned in the above analogy. They are a protective barrier against life's challenges as they make our journeys easier, safer, and more comfortable. Also, they help us navigate with greater efficiency and provide us with a steady supply of power.

But even when we are connected with our ancestors, we still have to maintain control over our lives and make the right turns when given proper direction. We likewise have to swerve to avoid potholes and debris on the road of life. We may even hit these objects from time to time or experience cracks on our windshield from flying objects along the way. However, our ancestors act as a protective barrier against such destructive forces. They cushion the blow so that we aren't completely overwhelmed by the impact.

To enjoy this level of protection and comfort when driving, we need to keep our vehicles tuned up and in good working condition. The same is true about maintaining a proper relationship with our ancestors. We must propitiate our ancestors through acts of veneration to keep our connection with them strong and in tack. Doing so keeps our relationship smooth and in proper working order so that we can effectively and efficiently live a destiny-driven life.

Fulfilling Your Destiny

The overriding purpose of connecting with your ancestors is to gain more insight into your destiny and how to successfully fulfill it. Of course, our ancestors assist us in many ways along our journey, but their ultimate goal is to help us remember why we are here on this earth. Because when we connect with our ancestors, we connect with ourselves.

Destiny refers to our soul mission or purpose. Our destinies are directly and inseparably connected to character development. Regardless of our mission on this earth, we are all charged with developing sound moral character to advance ourselves and future generations. Therefore, if you are not prepared to grow and develop on every level, you are approaching ancestor veneration for the wrong reasons.

Keep in mind that our destiny is not our occupation or career. We were not put on earth for the sole purpose of securing and maintaining employment. Though our destinies may be connected to our occupation, the two are not mutually exclusive. Our occupations may be essential vehicles to help us achieve our destinies, but they are never the sole reason for our earthly journey. When our occupation is attached to our destiny, it is simply a means to an end. And generally, the means is for connecting with specific people rather than for financial gain.

There are numerous examples of individuals whose destinies are strongly tied to their occupation. For example, Martin Luther King Jr. and Malcolm X were prominent religious leaders tasked with awakening and leading African Americans to a certain level of freedom and consciousness during the civil rights era.

These individuals earned their livelihood through their roles as religious leaders, and these positions served as major vehicles for them. Their leadership positions gave them access to and respect among large groups of people, which played a major role in gaining civil rights and liberties for African Americans.

These roles were also instrumental in elevating the consciousness of people throughout the African diaspora. However, they could have accomplished this same mission irrespective of their occupations. In fact, both of them are still accomplishing this mission through their legacy in the afterlife. Not to mention that many others have achieved this same soul mission without being directly connected to any form of religious or spiritual group.

Harriet Tubman was an express example of this. Her soul mission was also about leading her people to freedom during the slavery era. When she began her mission, she was a slave, which is not an occupation at all. Later, she served as a writer, spy, soldier, cook, nurse, and political activist. While these occupations assisted her in accomplishing her destiny, neither of them was connected with religion nor directly defined her soul purpose.

This indicates that everyone has a soul mission or destiny to achieve during their earthly sojourn. Some people are sent here to learn specific lessons. Others are meant to be profound leaders, prophets, healers, diviners, etc. Still, others are intended to preach, teach, or otherwise disseminate information. But regardless of our mission, we all need help with accomplishing it.

Our ancestors are charged with the task of assisting us with understanding our soul mission and with helping us accomplish this mission. Their assistance is available in many forms. They help to ensure our mental, physical, emotional, spiritual, financial, and social wellbeing. Also, they can and often do make our lives easier and more comfortable on many levels so that we can accomplish our soul mission.

But, keep in mind that our ancestors' primary goal is not necessarily to make us rich or remove all challenges or obstacles from our lives. Sometimes they are the ones who actually provoke us. While their lessons may seem harsh at times, they are taught from a place of love. Sometimes they have to use tough love to get us on track. In these instances, they may cause illness, sickness, financial problems, loss, etc., to get our attention. These aspects are discussed in more detail in a later chapter.

So don't assume that your life will automatically be easier or better once you begin venerating your ancestors. Conversely, you may have to put in more effort once you connect with your ancestors. You may even encounter periods of deep hardship, pain, and suffering before things get better in your life. But, know that everything you go through when you connect with your ancestors is for a divine purpose.

I know at least two individuals who overcame the generational pattern of extreme poverty through ancestor veneration. But the journey was not always smooth and easy for them. However, ancestral veneration significantly accelerated their path out of poverty. Once they started their veneration practice, their ancestors connected them to the right people and resources, which gave them the foundation for creating and generating wealth. After that, they lifted themselves and their families out of poverty through hard work, dedication, and good character.

While their ancestors assisted greatly in the process, these individuals had to follow the guidance they received, and they had to work hard to accomplish their goals. Neither of them experienced overnight success or achieved millionaire status (at least not to date). However, they both achieved steady and sustainable financial progress after connecting with their ancestors. They built their wealth and learned how to grow it in productive and effective ways. They have likewise learned many other beneficial lessons along the way, and they continue to grow in many areas of their lives as they continuously honor their ancestors.

Keep in mind that our ancestor's role in this process is ancillary to our own, as in the case with the previous examples. We bear the primary responsibility of carrying out our soul mission. We have to put in the work. In the examples I mentioned above, these individuals had to work hard to get themselves out of poverty. To be successful, they also had to exhibit good character and sound work ethics, including integrity, initiative, discipline, creativity, productivity, etc.

Money did not rain down from heaven for either of them. Instead, their ancestors put them in the right place at the right time, which allowed them to meet the right people and access the right resources. But they likewise had to have the right mindset, and they had to make the right choices to accomplish their goals. Ultimately, we have to work with our ancestors – they aren't meant to do all the heavy lifting.

Similar to these two individuals, our ancestors assist us in completing our soul mission through many other mechanisms including:

- Giving us wisdom and advice
- Helping us become self-aware
- Breaking generational curses
- Reconciling broken family ties
- Helping us develop empathy

Wisdom and Advice

Our ancestors accumulated a great deal of knowledge and wisdom when they were on this earthly plane. They have likewise continued to grow in wisdom since they have transitioned to the ancestral realm. Like many of our living elders, our ancestors want to impart their knowledge and wisdom unto us. They want to prevent us from making the same mistakes as they did. They also want to prevent us from making mistakes that they can foresee coming in the future.

Above all, they want us to make proper decisions that will aid us in fulfilling our destiny. When we make unnecessary mistakes, we can easily delay or forgo the fulfillment of our destiny. This is why our ancestors are constantly showing us the right path to take. They give us sage advice to help strengthen and replenish us that we may achieve sustainable growth and prosperity. Through this process, we are able to live a destiny-driven life.

Self-Awareness

Through ancestral veneration, you become more aware of where you came from and where you are going. As you cultivate a relationship with your ancestors, they will show you more about your heritage and lineage. Strong connections to your ancestral lineage are especially important for individuals throughout the African diaspora who were disconnected from their cultural identity through slavery and colonization.

Knowing where you came from helps you understand more about your behavioral patterns, your likes and dislikes, your personality, and many other aspects of your being. In understanding your roots and origin, you will better understand your purpose in life.

Despondently, many people throughout the African diaspora have been on a continuous and arduous journey trying to reconcile their identity. Due to the Transatlantic slave trade, many of us don't have direct knowledge of our heritage. These lost and broken familiar connections have resulted in many ills within the African diaspora community as we struggle to understand who we are and identify our purpose.

While DNA testing may give you some clues about your heritage, your ancestors can provide you with a wealth of information about your roots. In my personal experience, my ancestors literally took me on a journey around the world to explore my cultural heritage up close and in person. Through the travels that my ancestors orchestrated for me, I was able to see where they lived and how they interacted generations before I was born. This journey helped me understand why I think, speak, and act the way I do. It has been an enlightening journey that has also shown me how to fulfill my destiny.

Sense of Belonging

Just as when they were on earth, your ancestors want you to feel their love and affection for you. They can provide you with this same sense of belonging even in the afterlife by honoring their memory and communicating with them. As you develop a stronger relationship with them, you are able to "feel" their love and warmth permeating through your entire being.

This sensation is not spooky or scary. It is similar to the loving touch of a nurturing mother or the warm embrace of a doting father. In your time of need, your ancestors will show you that they are with you. Such a connection can be crucial for those who feel alone, neglected, or abandoned in life.

Breaking Generational Curses

Just like us, our ancestors were not perfect. Some of them did things that brought forth curses or negative energetic patterns that have perpetuated through our family lines. These patterns often result in behaviors that keep our family from progressing or prospering in specific ways.

In today's world, it is common to see generational habits of alcoholism, drug abuse, sex addiction, single-parenthood, divorce, incarceration, suicide, homelessness, underemployment, poverty, etc. Many of these generational behaviors are related to something that one or more of our family members set forth during their time on this earth. In which case, only our deceased loved ones have the keys to uncover the roots of these behaviors. As such, we need to seek their wisdom and guidance to find amicable solutions for overcoming these adverse energetic patterns. This is discussed in greater detail in the last chapter of this book.

Reconciliation

Ancestral veneration can be instrumental in helping us reconcile with both lost and living loved ones. Similar to and often because of generational curses, our family becomes disconnected. Resultantly, we may stop speaking to each other or purposefully do things to harm each other.

Broken family ties are never good because our family is our first line of defense in this realm and the afterlife. Sadly, we may cut off valuable family connections for very legitimate reasons such as molestation, incest, physical and mental abuse, etc. Obviously, if such behaviors persist, we need to distance ourselves from those who have or will potentially harm us. However, doing so does not heal the family members who are stuck in perpetuating such behaviors. As difficult as it may be, we need to seek reconciliation for these individuals to make our immediate and extended family whole.

You may have an ancestor who committed one of these atrocities against you or someone else in the family who wishes to reconcile the situation. Chances are whatever they did to you was likewise done to them. And, this pattern will continue until it is properly resolved. Ancestor veneration can provide the key to positive, long-lasting reconciliation in such cases.

Empathy

Being in constant communication with my ancestors has definitely helped to strengthen my sense of empathy toward them and others. I used to wonder why some of them made decisions that have resulted in life-altering ills and hardships for their descendants. However, as I started honoring my ancestors and their legacy (even when it was not so stellar), I have learned many valuable lessons about why they made such choices. I have realized that many of their unfortunate decisions came from a place of desperation and deprivation.

The majority of my most recent ancestors were part of the Transatlantic slavery system. As such, my ancestors often had to make do with what they had. Sometimes what they had at their disposal was not in their best interest or the best interest of our family line. However, they worked with what they had to resolve whatever challenge they were facing at the time.

Before I started my ancestor veneration practice, I used to get angry with them for their decisions. I often blamed them for the suffering that I have endured in my own life. While they held a level of responsibility for many of the subsequent hardships that my family and I have suffered, I have since learned that it was not their intention.

They have shown me why they made such decisions. They often did certain things because they felt like they had no other choice. And they were genuinely suffering at the time - not the type of temporary, easily-fixable suffering that we sometimes face in the modern world. They endured real suffering - going for days without adequate nourishment, being raped and abused, being degraded in many ways, working day and night in the cold and extreme heat, having no shelter, being separated from their family members, etc.

In some instances, they made poor decisions that have adversely impacted our entire family line. But they have since given me the knowledge and resources that I need to reconcile their actions so that my family can now experience many blessings. This knowledge has strengthened me and given me a greater level of empathy for them and others who had to make similar decisions.

Similarly, as you grow in this discipline, you will be able to empathize with your lost and living loved ones and others to a greater extent. You will be better able to see things from their perspective, which will help you be more patient, loving, and kind toward all living beings.

Which Ancestors are with You?

Our soul mission or destiny plays a vital role in determining which ancestors work with us. You probably have a specific set of ancestors in mind when you think about ancestor veneration. It is most likely the ancestors that you are most familiar with.

While some of these ancestors may be working with you, it is equally possible that they are not. More of your unknown ancestors might actually be working with you than those you knew or heard about through other family members. In fact, not knowing one or both sides of your lineage does not negate the fact that individuals from either side of your family may be guiding you. Even more, if you were adopted or otherwise reared by non-relatives, ancestors from your bloodline are still working with you though you may not be familiar with either side of your lineage. Also, keep in mind that the ancestors working with you can be from many generations before you.

The ancestors assigned to us are those we need the most in our journey. Notice that I stated *assigned* to us - not the other way around.

Though you may want to work with your maternal grandmother, she might not be the best ancestor to help you achieve your soul mission. If your destiny is to lead masses of people to a higher level of consciousness, your grandmother, who was a homemaker, may not be able to provide you with the best support in this endeavor. Instead, your great grandfather, who practiced Buddhism over 500 years ago, may have been assigned to work with you for this very reason.

So, keep this in mind as you honor your ancestors. Try not to be biased, and be sure to honor your known and unknown ancestors when practicing ancestor veneration. You won't always know all of the ancestors who are part of your spiritual team. Thus, if you honor your entire lineage, you will be duly respecting all of your ancestors. And, you will possibly tap into some resources that you never knew you had available to you.

The Importance of Intention

Before I dig deeper into the mechanics of ancestral veneration, I want to discuss the importance of intention in this process. Ancestor veneration or any other spiritual practice devoid of sound, resolute intention serves no real purpose. If you don't have good and benevolent intentions when performing spiritual rituals, your efforts will either be fruitless or counter-productive.

Intention is the goal, purpose, or targeted outcome of something. When engaging in ancestral veneration, your intention should be virtuous. Consider that from a medicinal perspective, one meaning of intention defines this concept as "the process of healing a wound." That's very powerful! Because it indicates that the ultimate goal of intention is to alleviate, relieve, or mitigate rather than exacerbate an injury or lesion.

If we apply this same definition to the practice of ancestor veneration, our primary goal in this process should be to achieve healing or relief. Healing can and should be sought in every area of our lives whenever we honor our ancestors. This includes our physical, mental, emotional, spiritual, financial, and social well-being. When done to achieve holistic healing, ancestor veneration can be an extraordinarily potent tool.

The goal of honoring your ancestors should never be strictly for self-serving purposes. Your ancestors are not your personal genie in a bottle. While they are available to help you in many aspects of your life, you should not come to them only when you need things and never give anything in return. You should also never engage in this practice to harm others. Whenever you honor your ancestors, your intentions should be pure and clear. Otherwise, you risk inviting evil and malevolent spirits into your space that can cause you more harm than good.

Chapter 3: How to Connect with Your Ancestors

The first step to developing a relationship with your ancestors requires you to initiate the process. Your ancestors have been with you throughout your entire life. However, you can't have a strong relationship with them if you have not taken the necessary steps to connect with them. Communication is a two-way process.

There are many ways to connect with your ancestors. No one way is inherently right or wrong. It's all about what works for you and your ancestors. However, if your ancestors request that you honor them in a specific way, you should make every attempt to do so. Otherwise, you should never feel compelled to do something that doesn't work or feel right for you.

Most connection pathways are pretty straightforward. Our ancestors are not complicated - they simply want to be acknowledged and properly reverenced. When they receive honor, respect, and attention from us, they are more inspired to do things for us. Otherwise, they will simply do the bare minimum that they are assigned to do.

Energy conduits are used for venerating ancestors as they create a pathway for spirits to project themselves into the earthly realm. For this reason, the four elements are essential in ancestral rituals and ceremonies. They provide a source of energy in which the ancestors can connect to the earthly realm.

In this section, I discuss several tools and techniques that are effective for communicating with your ancestors. You can implement some or all of these methods. Whatever you choose to do, do not overwhelm yourself by doing too much at once or trying to do something beyond your reach. Your ancestors want to connect with you, but they understand your limitations.

If you are low on cash, get what you can afford. As you grow in your relationship with your ancestors, they will provide you with the resources you need for more elaborate or higher-level veneration ceremonies. However, if you have the resources to purchase more or higher-quality items for conducting ancestral veneration ceremonies, you need to do so. Don't skim if you don't have to. Of course, exercise financial wisdom and common sense when purchasing items or services to honor your ancestors. But, give your ancestors the best that you can afford.

Remember, what you put into the practice is what you will get out of it. This is related to your money, time, and effort. Your time and effort are just as important as your money. You could essentially pour a lot of money into the process but give little time and effort to it. And vice versa. So, if you give them meager ceremonies when you can do better, you will receive meager blessings in return.

Ancestor Altars

Ancestor altars are a mainstay in ancestral veneration. They are one of the primary tools we use to connect with our ancestors in the physical realm. While most people think of a dedicated space filled with spiritual tools when referencing a spiritual shrine of this nature, there are actually two types of ancestor altars.

First, it is essential to understand that you are an ancestral altar in your own right. You embody your ancestors' DNA and epigenetic traits, which means that you are, in essence, your ancestors. Your physical body serves as an altar in which your ancestors commune with you on a continuous basis. This is why you must take proper care of yourself because you are effectively taking care of your ancestors when you do so. Maintaining your well-being is actually one form of ancestor veneration that I will discuss later in this chapter.

However, in this section, I am referring to an external space dedicated to ancestral spirits. Such a space serves as a focal point for you and your ancestors. It is a place where you can meditate on the memories of your ancestors. Likewise, it is an area where your ancestors can congregate when you spend time with them or give them offerings.

There are many great resources available for learning how to set up an ancestor altar. I discuss some of the basics in this section. As you read my recommendations, note that you can keep your altar as simple or as complicated as you wish. You don't need to spend a lot of money to build your ancestor altar. It is also not necessary to furnish it all at once. Ancestor altars tend to be a work in progress for the average person. The most important thing about an ancestor altar is the energy you put into creating and maintaining it.

The first thing you need to determine is what will serve as the base or foundation of your altar. You don't need an entire room dedicated to your ancestor altar - although you can use a whole room for your altar. Typically, a table, stand, container, window seal, wall mount, closet, drawer, chest, etc., will do the trick if you set it up correctly. On the other hand, you do need to be concerned about the material composition of the base. It is best to select something with a surface made from natural materials such as wood, glass, stone, clay, etc. Synthetic materials are not conducive to connecting with the spirit realm.

Next, you need to decide where you plan to place your altar. I recommend keeping it in a low-traffic area whenever possible. An ancestor altar is an intimate tool that deserves respect and reverence. Keeping it in common areas with high traffic can disrupt the flow and energy of your ancestors in the altar space.

It is also commonly recommended to keep altars out of bedroom and bathroom spaces. These are areas that require the greatest level of privacy. It is not a good idea to invite ancestors into such spaces because of the types of activities that generally occur in bedrooms and bathrooms. However, if you don't have a more appropriate place to put your altar, you can set it up in your bedroom and use a partition to section off the area. Doing so will give you a greater level of privacy. The same applies to placing it in a bathroom if you live in studio-style living quarters without partisans. There are several ways to address privacy issues if this is a concern for you.

If your entire family uses the altar, it may be necessary to keep it in a common area. Even in such cases, I still recommend keeping it away from the prying eyes of guests or visitors who may not understand or may be opposed to it. A shared common area less frequented by guests may be the best place to keep an altar for use by your entire family. Your ancestor altar is not and should not be open to scrutiny of any kind. It is a sacred, personal artifact similar to a journal that should be protected and guarded at all times.

Items for Your Ancestor Altar

Once you have selected a base and location for your altar, you need to choose the items you wish to place on it. But, before placing items on your ancestor altar, be sure to clean all the surfaces of the table, stand, etc., that you plan to use for the base of your altar. You can do this using water, alcohol, or spiritual colognes (more on this in the next section). If you wish to cover the base of your altar, you can place a white cloth on the top of it. White represents and attracts pure and clean energy, which is the type of energy that you want to invite into your altar space.

However, a cloth is not absolutely necessary if your base has a natural surface such as wood. Though, I recommend using lighter color wood surfaces for the same purpose as using a white cloth. It is best to use something that attracts clean, high vibrational energy when working with your ancestors.

Everything that you place on your altar should have meaning and purpose. Most of the items you use should be personal and unique to you and your ancestors. However, certain things are fundamental to any ancestor altar. These include the four elements – fire, earth, air, and water. Each of the elements represents the foundational forces apparent in the natural world. These are vital forces necessary for sustaining life on earth as they operate within all living beings.

Fire represents passion, motivation, inspiration, movement, etc., or the essence (àṣẹ) of life – it energizes and strengthens us. Earth represents the material world that provides us with security and safety – it effectively sustains our physical, mental, financial, and social well-being. Air correlates to the mind and intellectual capabilities – it is the driving force behind our thoughts and ability to communicate with all beings. Water coincides with our emotions and intuition – it cleanses us and gives us clarity, renewal, and refreshment.

Table 3-1 outlines some common items you can use to represent the four elements on your altar. Don't feel compelled to use them all - select what works best for you.

Element	Items
Air (East)	Feathers, incense smoke, images or icons of spiritual beings or flying animals
Water (West)	Water, coffee, tea, non-alcoholic liquids
Earth (North)	Crystals, stones, rocks, herbs, coins, dirt, soil, sand, salt
Fire (South)	Candles, charcoal, incense, alcohol

Table 3-1: Symbolism of the Four Elements & Directions

You can also represent the four elements by placing a cross or ankh on your altar. If you don't feel comfortable using a cross because of its affiliation with Christianity, keep in mind that early spiritualists who pre-date Christianity used the cross in their spiritual ceremonies and rituals. It was used in ancient Egypt

(Kemet) and Ethiopia (Nubia) centuries before the advent of modern Christianity.

Throughout history, the cross has symbolized the four directions, which likewise correlate to the four elements. Dispersed throughout the East African region, one of the most ancient civilizations known to modern-day man, ancient crosses can still be found in this area today. So, you can effectively incorporate this directional element into your altar without associating it with a specific religious practice. Simply use a cross without Christian imagery, or use an ankh, as it serves the same purpose.

Another essential feature to include on your ancestor altar is a representation of the four directions (east, west, north, and south). The four directions correspond to the four elements as outlined in Table 3-1. Specific spirits live in and rule over each direction. Therefore, paying homage to the four directions is likewise elemental in ancestor veneration.

Keep in mind that Table 3-1 outlines one representation of the symbolism or correlation of the four directions. Other references may categorize them differently. Feel free to use the symbology that best resonates with you when determining which source is most accurate.

Additional elements that you may want to use on your altar are images of lost loved ones. Be careful not to place pictures of living people on the altar. If your photos include living and deceased people, you can crop out the living people using photo editing software. You can likewise make a photo-quality copy of the picture and physically cut out the image(s) of the people who are still living.

Other standard items usually placed on ancestor altars include things that belonged to lost loved ones. If you have your grandmother's favorite pearls or your grandfather's cherished watch, you can add these items to your altar. The essence of your ancestors still lingers on these items, so they are great ways to connect with your ancestors.

If you don't have items that belonged to your ancestors, you can use items that represent your ancestors or their culture. For instance, coins, artwork, jewelry, clothing, dried herbs, or other items from areas in which your ancestors are from are great additions to an ancestor altar. It is best to place culturally specific items on your altar for the sake of authenticity. For instance, if you have Ghanian heritage, beads, money, cloth, or other items distinct to this country are best to use rather than similar items from various parts of Africa.

Adding cultural paraphernalia to your altar is a great way to remember and embrace your cultural heritage. Every time you look at these items, you will remember your roots. They will remind you of where your ancestors came from and what they went through during their journey on earth.

If your ancestors practiced a particular religion or form of spirituality, you could also add the holy book(s) of that religion or faith to your altar. Even if you don't practice or believe in the religion, your ancestors will be greatly honored by this gesture. The goal is to show appreciation for your heritage, even if it is against your current belief systems.

Alcohol is often included on ancestor altars because it likewise acts as a conduit for spirits. It is actually a form of energy that serves as a channel for conveying spiritual energy. This is where the phrase "wine and spirits" comes from. However, if you or your family have a history of alcoholism, I discourage adding alcohol to an ancestor altar. You can work with this element in less threatening or enticing forms, which I will discuss later in the next section.

It may also be helpful to include a sound-maker such as a bell or a rattler on the altar. Such devices are often used to call forth spirits during ceremonies or rituals. They aren't necessary but can be beneficial when working at your altar. These are just some of the many items that can be placed on an ancestor altar. The ultimate goal is to create a space where you and your ancestors feel comfortable interacting with each other.

Working with Your Ancestor Altar

Once you have your altar set up, you can and should begin working with it. As I mentioned before, an ancestral altar is supposed to serve as a focal point for communication with your ancestors. It is not meant to be just another piece of decor in your home.

It is also good to cleanse it with Florida water or another spiritual cologne on a regular basis. With these concoctions, you can effectively clear a space of negative energy, purify an environment, and relieve anxiety and stress. Your altar should be cleaned frequently to prevent the build-up of foul or stagnant energy. A weekly, bi-weekly, or monthly cleansing schedule is generally sufficient to maintain clean energy in your altar space.

If you keep water on your altar, you should also change it regularly. Water acts as a portal through which spirits travel. Water also represents the fluidity of the relationship between you and your ancestors. It is a basic essential for an ancestor altar, as previously mentioned. But, if it is dirty or cloudy, it has the opposite effect – it attracts unclean energies and causes blockages. At a bare minimum, it is best to change the water weekly. When you add new water to the altar, you should use a clean vessel to store it in. If you plan to use the same glass, simply wash it before refilling it with water.

Ideally, an ancestor altar should be blessed with an intention prayer before you begin working with it. An intention prayer sets the tone for how you plan to use the altar space. This prayer serves to invite your ancestors into the altar space and tells them why you set it up. I encourage you to speak from your heart when you pray or talk to your ancestors. However, you can use this simple prayer below or consult a prayer book to help you find the right words:

> *Ancestors, known and unknown, I invite you into this space to connect with me. I have set up this altar for us to develop and grow a loving, long-lasting relationship. This altar serves as a memorial space and place of honor for you. As we walk this journey together, let me know how I can best honor you in this space as I want it to be inviting and pleasing to you.*

As mentioned, the prayer above is very basic and straightforward. Use it as a template to fill in your own words from your heart. When I set up my altar, my prayers were more elaborate and personal than those in the template above. I talked to my ancestors about every object that I put on the altar as I explained the significance and meaning of each item. I did this when I initially set up my altar, and I likewise do it each time I add something to my altar.

For instance, some of the last objects added to my altar were a couple of Dan masks from West African. The masks are sacred artifacts used in traditional religious practices to communicate with the spirit world. So, I informed my ancestors that I added the masks to their altar to memorialize my West African heritage. I let them know that the masks were placed on the altar to honor our lineage and symbolize my commitment to renew our cultural heritage.

This is just one example of how I introduce new items to my altar. If you choose this method, keep in mind that it can be time-consuming if you have several objects to place at one time. Therefore, allot enough time for this activity so that you don't rush through the process. If you bring that type of energy to your altar, you will create the same type of energic pattern between you and your ancestors. If you want them to be patient and gentle when they assist you, you should interact with them in a like manner. They don't want to feel like an afterthought or burden to you, just as you don't want to feel like you are one to them. Remember, you will attract the same type of energy that you bring to your altar.

After you cleanse and pray over your altar, you can begin doing many activities there. It is a great place to talk to the ancestors, sing, listen to high vibrational music, meditate, visualize, offer prayers of gratitude, speak affirmations, laugh, cry, reminisce, read, study, etc. Any form of positive introspective activity is generally acceptable to the ancestors. They simply want to spend quality, meaningful time with you, and they want to be remembered.

There are no set parameters of when or how long you should interact with your ancestors at the altar. Spending time at my ancestor altar is a daily practice for me. However, such a schedule doesn't work for everyone. You may only have time for weekly, bi-weekly, monthly, etc., sessions at your ancestor altar.

However, I discourage you from setting up an ancestor altar if you don't plan to interact with it regularly. Otherwise, what is the point? An abandoned or neglected altar only serves to attract negative energy. So, if you are not interested in inviting such energy into your space, it is best not to set up an ancestor altar if you don't plan to attend to and clean it regularly.

The more time you spend at your altar, the stronger your connection will get. However, do keep in mind that you need to spend enough quality time with the living as well. Try not to overdo it to the point where you spend more time with your ancestors than with your living family members and friends. Your ancestors appreciate your dedication and devotion to them, but they want you to have a blessed and fruitful life as well. They know that you need a proper and balanced relationship with them and other living beings in your environment for this to happen.

In conclusion, you can do all or most of your spiritual work at your ancestor altar. Offerings are commonly given at the ancestor altar. I will discuss this topic in more detail in the next section. Many of the other practices mentioned throughout the rest of this section can also be performed at your ancestral altar. This is why an altar can be an integral part of connecting with your ancestors.

Giving Offerings

Many people who have knowledge of or experience with Christianity are familiar with the concept of offerings. Offerings are also commonly given when petitioning a higher power or deity for a request. The idea of giving offerings is founded on the principles of gratitude and reciprocity. We give offerings to show our appreciation for blessings that we have received and as a form of "payment" for the blessings we anticipate receiving from answered prayer requests.

This same concept applies to giving offerings to ancestors. We give offerings to show our appreciation and understanding of the reciprocal nature of giving and receiving. As the expression goes, *there is nothing free in the spirit realm.* If you get something without giving in return, this leaves a void that must be filled. If the void is not filled through the process of reciprocity, it will be filled with ill will or bad luck. This same principle applies in the earthly realm. How much more in the spiritual realm - as above, so below.

Ancestors do not ask for things because they need them for survival. Instead, they require offerings for energy exchange. For them to interact with us in the earthly realm, they need the conditions to be conducive. In other words, they need an energy source to attach to for connecting with us on a deeper level.

So, when you invite them into your space, you must give them an energy conduit such as water, alcohol, candles, incense, etc. These types of portals allow them to operate with greater power and speed in your life. There are many forms of offerings that you can give. However, heat, steam, and smoke are some of the most effective conduits. They serve as hot channels for spiritual energy, which is conducive to fast action or quick movement.

In the following section, you will find offerings commonly given to ancestors during veneration ceremonies and rituals. Each of these elements has distinct and beneficial properties that can be useful in different ways.

Whenever you give an offering, it is best to say an intention prayer before doing so. Like the prayer I mentioned previously, you need to state the purpose or meaning of the offering. For example, you can say, "I present you with this glass of water as it represents purity, flow, and prosperity. I offer it to you as a portal that we may have clear and consistent communication."

Candles and Incense

Candles and incense both embody the elements of fire and air when burned. Fire and air attract and give energy to spirits, as already mentioned. It is vital to use them appropriately when giving them as offerings. White candles are the standard in all ancestral-based work. Shades of white, such as cream, eggshell, ivory, vanilla, etc., are acceptable if you don't have access to pure white. However, I don't recommend using other colors when working with ancestors, especially not dark colors. It is best to forgo candles if you can't find the right color because you don't want to invite the wrong types of energy.

Specific incense and resins like frankincense and myrrh attract ancestral spirits. Frankincense promotes relaxation and has a calming effect, while myrrh detoxifies and purifies. Used in combination, these resins can clear dead, stagnant, and negative energy in an environment. Simultaneously, they support a relaxed, calm atmosphere for engaging in spiritual work. When activated with fire, they serve as an invitation for your ancestors to come into a particular space or environment. Other fragrances and resins are also used in various cultures for ancestral work. It is best to select varieties that correspond to your cultural heritage.

Candles and incense can be activated whenever you engage in ancestral work. You can light them each time you go to the altar, even if you do so multiple times a day. You can also burn them once a day or weekly, even if you engage with your altar several times a day. Do what works best for your budget and lifestyle.

Food

Many people give their ancestors food offerings. While it is a beautiful gesture and show of appreciation, it should be handled with careful consideration. Food is an energy source, which attracts ancestral spirits. However, always be mindful of the type of food you give and when and how you dispose of it.

Generally, living foods are excellent choices for our ancestors. Living foods carry a higher vibration than cooked foods. Fruits are ideal offerings because they are sweet and maintain a high vibration in their natural state. However, cooked meals carry a certain layer of authenticity and cultural connection that is likewise beneficial. When cooking meals for your ancestors, you can share a portion of your meals with them or cook something special for them.

If you give your ancestors cooked food, be sure it is something they liked when they were alive. In today's world, vegan, vegetarian, and alternative diets are ubiquitous. However, we have to keep in mind that many of our ancestors consumed meat, fish, poultry, etc. Even more, those who may have enjoyed a primarily plant-based diet didn't generally consume the types of food that we now consider to be vegan or vegetarian.

As such, if you decide to cook for your ancestors, you should cook meals that they would have actually enjoyed. Remember, the offering is for them and not for you. Suppose you have ethical, spiritual, philosophical, or other aversions to preparing the types of foods that your ancestors ate. In that case, it is best not to give them cooked food offerings. You can simply give them fresh fruits and vegetables as an amicable compromise.

Also, keep in mind that whatever food offerings you present to them should have a purpose. Even when cooking their favorite foods, you should select foods that hold significance and meaning in some way. This concept is similar to the observation of Passover in the Bible. The annual feast of Passover was ordained to commemorate when the Most High passed over the children of Israel and killed all the firstborn of Egypt to provoke the Pharaoh to let the Israelites go. Therefore, the Israelites were instructed to maintain an annual feast unto the Most High as a way of remembering this event.

Every part of the meal held significance and purpose. The lamb represented the sacrificial lamb that they offered for protection against the Most High's wrath. The bitter herbs symbolized the bitterness that the Israelites experienced during their sojourn in Egypt.

And symbolism was assigned to the rest of the meal in kind.

It is beneficial to prepare meals for your ancestors in a similar manner. Every part of the meal should have significance. It doesn't need to have deep meaning like the Passover meal, but each part of the meal should serve a purpose. You may use your grandmother's fried chicken recipe because that was everyone's favorite. Or, you could make your mother's sweet peach cobbler because it reminds you of your family's summer gatherings in the south.

When you present food to your ancestors, it should be given on a white plate or bowl. Enamelware is commonly used for this purpose as it embodies the vibe of the old times. Whatever dish you choose, you should reserve it strictly for the use of feeding your ancestors. Avoid using it for other purposes, if possible.

You can give food offerings as frequently as you desire. Just be sure that doing so doesn't become a burden. Otherwise, you may become indignant and frustrated after so long. Weekly food offerings are the standard in many cultures. However, you can do it as frequently as you desire. Some people give their ancestors daily, monthly, quarterly, or annual food offerings.

You can place food offerings on your ancestor altar, outside, or in other locations. Perishable food offerings should only be left on the altar for a few days. You can leave unpeeled fruits such as oranges or apples for longer periods. Food for your ancestors should never be left to spoil or rot on their altar or other dedicated space in your home.

Humans should never consume ancestral offerings. It is best to discard food offerings when removing them from an altar or other space. If you have issues with throwing away food, you can leave the offering under a tree when you remove it from your home. Animals generally consume offerings that are initially or subsequently placed outside. Thus, it is best to leave food offerings far away from residential or commercial dwellings. Forests or wooded areas are generally better places for leaving such offerings.

Coffee

Coffee is commonly given as an offering in ancestral rituals and ceremonies. This aromatic drink has significant meaning in the spiritual realm. Due to its high caffeine content, coffee acts as a potent stimulant - it initiates and maintains a wakeful state. It has a similar effect when used as a conduit for connecting with our ancestors.

Typically offered once a week in many spiritual traditions, coffee keeps our relationship with our ancestors strong, alert, and lively. Sugar is often added to this stimulant as a gesture of maintaining a sweet, amicable relationship with our lost loved ones.

When offering coffee to your ancestors, it should be appropriately filtered and served piping hot. The steam from the heat serves as a channel for transmuting spiritual energy. It is best to prepare your ancestor's favorite brand of coffee for such offerings. If you don't know what brand they liked, try to find a coffee derived from their native homeland. Otherwise, you can buy whatever brands are available to you in your local area.

As mentioned, properly filter the coffee through a coffee maker or other appliance designed for this purpose. Once the coffee is ready, add some sugar (generally 3-4 teaspoons is sufficient) and place it on your ancestor altar. Speak to your ancestors and tell them that you are offering the coffee to them, tell them why you are offering the coffee, and explain the significance of each component of the coffee.

Typically, you can leave coffee offerings out for one to three days. You never want it to grow mold or start to mildew. If small children or animals can access the coffee, you may want to place the coffee on a high, sturdy table to avoid spills or unintentional human or animal consumption of the coffee. You can discard the remaining portion or use it in a spiritual bath when you finish with the coffee offering. Ancestor offerings should not be consumed internally.

Gratitude

You should also offer your ancestors prayers of gratitude and thanksgiving. You can say, write about, or meditate on the things you are grateful for. Expressing gratitude for something they did while they were alive or since they have passed on is acceptable. You can also give thanksgiving for specific blessings that you have received from them.

For instance, I often tell my ancestors that I am grateful that they pressed through the hardships that they endured. By doing so, they have paved the way for my family and me to enjoy a better life. I also thank them for continuing to give me wisdom in my day-to-day journey.

Gratitude is best served hot. It can and should be expressed in the moment that you feel appreciation for something your ancestors did for you. Also, offer gratitude when you are genuinely thankful. You can reserve specific days or times for giving gratitude prayers. However, it is much better to do so when you truly feel grateful. It should not feel like a chore or simply be lip service. Keep in mind that our ancestors can easily recognize when we are not honest or genuine.

Flowers

Flowers have a unique history in relation to death. Before the advent of modern embalming and body preservation techniques, dead bodies often carried a foul stench even after they were embalmed. In order to prevent funeral attendees from being offended by these odors, flowers were used to mask the unpleasant smells of decaying bodies.

Since that time, flowers have played an integral role in death, burial, and memorial rites. We often take flowers to individuals on their sickbed. We likewise take flowers to the funeral home or burial site during wake and funeral ceremonies. And it is common to include flowers in memorial services immediately and years after a person's death. In this way, flowers have become symbols of love, honor, respect, and remembrance rather than deodorizers. In this same vein, it is acceptable and appropriate to give flowers as part of ancestral veneration rituals.

You can place flower offerings on your ancestor altar, at the grave of your ancestors, in a nearby cemetery, or other amenable location. White flowers are typically given as ancestral offerings. However, you can also offer your ancestors some of their favorite varieties. Flowers can be provided for ancestors on a weekly, monthly, bi-annual, annual basis, etc. However, if you are giving live flowers, be sure that they are fresh, not dry, old, or withered. Once they begin to die, it is best to remove them from the offering space.

Music

Music is one of my favorite offerings to my ancestors. It is a meditative practice that helps me connect with them on a deep, soulful level. Music can likewise be a simple and delightful offering for both you and your ancestors. The first thing you need to do is select the right music. As with all things when dealing with your ancestors, the music you choose should always be high vibrational. This means that it should have clean, uplifting, inspiring lyrics and tones. Otherwise, you risk attracting negative or low vibrational energies. Also, your ancestors may be offended by certain types of music, so be mindful when choosing music for your ancestors.

In general, the music that you select should be something that your ancestors enjoyed listening to when they were alive. Remember, the offering is for them, not you. So, even if you are not particularly fond of the music they listened to, you should not deprive them of it. You can play all types of music, including gospel, jazz, reggae, soul, blues, classical, etc., for your ancestors. Try to curate a list of songs that your ancestors truly enjoyed from their era. Ask some of your living relatives if you don't remember or are unsure what types of music your ancestors enjoyed.

It is relatively easy to find music dating back to the 1920s or beyond online. You can download the songs and add them to a playlist. If you have the gift of music, you can likewise sing or play an instrument for your ancestors.

Once you have selected the music, determine when and where you will play it for your ancestors. Again, your ancestor altar is usually the perfect place for this type of activity.

However, if your altar is in a high-traffic area, you may want to find a quieter space. Lakes, beaches, forests, and other natural spaces are also great places to present music offerings. But do be mindful of other people if you choose to give a music offering in public. Also, consider your privacy needs when offering music in public spaces.

Once you have found your location, make yourself comfortable. Pull out your music and tell your ancestors that you are offering the music to them. Then, get comfortable and listen to the music with them or serenade them. There is no specific amount of time that you need to spend engaged in this process.

The goal is to spend time reflecting on who your ancestors were, where they have been, and what they have gone through. Also, it is important to simply enjoy sharing part of their history with them. This is why listening to music from their era is more effective. The words and sounds of the music make it easier to reminisce about them and reflect on their past.

Listening to high vibrational music is a calming, meditative practice. I often experience peace and rejuvenation whenever I offer music to my ancestors. This is another benefit of giving offerings – doing so can positively impact your overall health and well-being. In particular, listening to the music of your ancestors can conjure memories of the times that you spent with them. Some of the memories may be happy, yet others may be sad. But even the painful memories are instrumental in the healing process.

Libations

Libations are another form of offering that you can give to your ancestors. While typically thought of as alcohol, libations can come in many forms. A libation is any type of drink (and sometimes food) that can be poured as a ritual offering to a spirit. In African spiritual systems, it is common to pour libations in memory of the dead.

In fact, this tradition made its way into hip-hop culture in the 1990s. A few music videos featured urban youths pouring alcoholic drinks in memory of their deceased friends (homies). While some people categorized this as ghetto during that period, it was actually a form of ancestor veneration derived from an age-old practice still honored by cultures from around the world.

Elders of traditional African spiritual systems generally pour libations. This honor is likewise reserved for the males in many African societies. However, it is acceptable for almost any competent, responsible adult to pour libations to recognize their ancestors in the western world.

Aside from alcohol, libations may include water, milk, olive oil, honey, ghee, beer, and traditional wine. Some cultures even pour solid substances like rice, cornmeal, flour, etc. Strong liquor such as white rum, dry gin, vodka, etc., are typically used when pouring alcohol-based libations. These types of drinks are associated with waking or rousing the spirits, requesting protection, and purification. It is best to use the substance that you are most comfortable with when pouring libations. If you or your family have a strong history of alcoholism, you may want to avoid using alcohol when pouring libations.

Once you have chosen and prepared your libation offering, decide where you want to pour it. These offerings are typically drizzled on the ground in soil, dirt, or sand. If these elements are not easily accessible to you in nature, you can purchase soil and place it in a pot for plants. This soil can then be used during your libation offerings. If you are only pouring water libations, you can also use a potted plant for this purpose. I don't recommend pouring alcohol libations in potted plants as it may kill them.

Libations are typically offered in droplets or trickles rather than in large spouts. While pouring the libations, prayers are said to the ancestors to invoke their presence or ask for a specific request. These rituals can be done on a daily, weekly, monthly, or annual basis, etc. If you practice within a tradition, it is best to consult an elder or mentor to determine how to best honor your culture when offering libations.

Time

Your time is a precious commodity to your ancestors. As with the living, quality time is much more valuable than material things. Yes, you will spend time with your ancestors if you engage in the practices I have already mentioned. However, most of your time is spent preparing and engaging in those activities rather than simply communicating with your ancestors.

So be sure to give your ancestors plenty of your time. You can do many things when spending time with your ancestors. Chief among the things you should be doing is talking to them. Talk to them about your life and let them know when you are happy, sad, excited, discouraged, etc. Talk to your ancestors and talk to them often.

You can have a conversation with them just like you do with the living. Simply pull out a comfortable seat and have a friendly chat with your ancestors. It won't cost you anything of material value, but this gesture will be greatly rewarding to you and your ancestors.

Memorial Services and Activities

Remembering your ancestors and their legacy is another way to honor them. When you speak well of your ancestors in your day-to-day conversations or make mention of their accomplishments, this is pleasing to them. There are also a number of other ways that you can memorialize your ancestors.

Aside from honoring their names and legacy through praise, you can also name people and things after them. For instance, you can name your child(ren) the same first or middle name as some of your cherished loved ones. In this way, you are continuously honoring their legacy through their namesake.

You can also give donations, set up scholarships, entitle buildings or business units, etc., in their name or legacy. Bestowing such honor to your ancestors allows their legacy to live on for generations. Hosting family gatherings such as reunions is yet another way to honor their legacy. These types of meetings are perfect for reminiscing over photos or videos, passing along family history to the next generation, pouring libations, having moments of silence for the dearly departed, etc.

Another meaningful way you can keep the memory of your ancestors alive is by maintaining their graves. If you know and have access to the burial site of your ancestors, you should maintain it on a regular basis. You can visit their graves at scheduled times throughout the year to clean them and bring fresh flowers or other offerings. When visiting a gravesite, be careful not to disturb the peace of the cemetery. Remember that other people are buried there who likewise have the right to rest in peace.

Elevation Prayers and Rituals

As I mentioned in the first chapter, all of our lost loved ones did not live the best lives when they were on earth. Some of them committed egregious, vile, and harmful acts. This may have even been a lifestyle for a few of them.

These individuals are typically not elevated to ancestor status when they depart this earth because of their lifestyle. The same is true for those who commit suicide. They can't be promoted to ancestor status because they chose to leave this realm rather than complete their soul mission. Instead, these individuals exist in a state of perpetual torture, which many religious people refer to as hell. However, I am not referring to the hell often associated with Abrahamic religions. Though, some of our lost loved ones are definitely in a state of misery, torment, and agony.

While hell is both a mental and physical space, it has more to do with one's state of mind than anything else. Because of the things they did while on earth, they usually don't feel worthy of achieving ancestor status. So, they submit themselves to lower-level energies that cause them to remain in a perpetual state of torture.

Other lost loved ones remain earthbound after their spirit leaves their body. This phenomenon can occur for several reasons. It is common when people die sudden or violent deaths and are unaware of their demise. Individuals who are murdered also tend to linger on the earth - many want to avenge their death before they fully transition to the astral realm. Others may become earthbound when they are too attached to their earthly life and simply refuse to move on.

Neither of these conditions has to be a permanent state of existence for your lost loved ones. You can assist them in their elevation process through prayers and rituals. In many African spiritual systems, elevation is a common rite of passage for anyone who departs this earth. Many people who practice traditional spirituality elevate their dearly departed as soon as they pass away.

You can and should likewise say elevation prayers for your lost loved ones if you are concerned about their well-being in the afterlife. And you can even incorporate rituals during your prayer sessions to make your prayers official. This process is not much different from saying "rest in peace" or "rest in power" to the dearly departed. The sentiment is the same - the difference is your intention. While many recite this phrase out of habit, you are mindfully, thoughtfully, and deliberately assisting your lost loved ones in the ascension process whenever you purposefully say elevation prayers and conduct corresponding rituals. Elevation prayer and ritual ceremonies can be conducted after the transition of any of your lost loved ones. You can also do this at any time when performing elevation rituals for all of your lost loved ones. You should include your known and unknown relatives in such ceremonies.

However, it is customary to wait at least one year and one day before engaging in such prayers or rituals in some traditions. This waiting period is generally instituted to give the dearly departed time to orient to their new environment. If they aren't aware of where they are or refuse to leave, your prayers and rituals will be ineffective.

There are many ways to say elevation prayers and conduct ceremonies for your lost loved ones. If you practice a specific tradition, I suggest that you start there. Many traditional spiritual practices have special rituals for elevating the deceased. Elders in these traditional systems can generally guide adherents in conducting elevation ceremonies according to their lineage.

If you don't practice a tradition, you can say a prayer while presenting coffee or another offering to your ancestors and to the deceased members of your family who you wish to elevate. First, start by lighting a white candle and giving a coffee offering to your ancestors. Place these items on a table specifically dedicated to them. Also, put a clear glass of water on the table. Then, invite your ancestors into the sacred space and ask them for their assistance as you complete your elevation prayer. Also, ask them to protect you from any evil or negative forces that may try to enter your space as you complete your prayer.

Next, call the names of all of your known deceased relatives from both sides of your family. You only need to say the names of individuals from your direct lineage (parents, grandparents, great-grandparents, etc.). You can also write this on a piece of paper and place it on the table with the candle, coffee, and water.

Once you have called upon your ancestors, you can then say a prayer to elevate your deceased loved ones. The following elements are most commonly used in such prayers:

- Call upon the Higher Spirit you serve and ask this force to forgive your deceased loved ones of their misdeeds.
- Offer love, light, and compassion to these souls for the misdeeds that they committed while on earth. List their misdeeds if you are aware of them.
- Offer your forgiveness to the stuck souls of your family lineage, especially if any of them did something to harm or hurt you while they

were alive. With a sincere heart, let them know that you no longer hold them accountable for their misdeeds.

- Ask that these souls be permitted to elevate in love and light that they may serve the living in practical and beneficial ways.
- Close the prayer by commanding all blocked and harmful energic patterns caused by the misdeeds of these souls to be released and removed from your bloodline.

The information outlined above is a simple template for conducting an elevation prayer and ceremony for your lost loved ones. You can make it as elaborate as you desire. Nine-day ancestor elevation ceremonies are common within some spiritual practices. They often include food offerings, singing, dancing, and other elements in the ritual.

If you need more guidance, you can also ask your ancestors to show you how to effectively conduct an elevation ceremony. They should be able to guide you to the best practices that are most effective for your bloodline. Keep in mind that the most important thing is that you are sincere while completing this process.

Family Relationships

Maintaining intact cohesive family relationships is a critical and meaningful way to honor our ancestors. Our ancestors want a unified family because they know this is the key to their descendants' sustained growth, maturation, and development. It is also the first layer of defense in a wounded world.

Contrarily, broken families are often a source of shame, guilt, and embarrassment. Broken families tend to suffer more in their health, finances, relationships, and other major life areas, which ultimately leads to arrested development and stunted growth.

Broken people are usually riddled with emotional baggage and hang-ups, which makes it difficult for them to enjoy a productive and successful life. This level of brokenness often results in negative behavior patterns that lead to imprisonment, poverty, addictions, and the like. These types of behavioral patterns create more work for our ancestors. Instead of enjoying a harmonious, easy-going relationship with their progeny, they are constantly trying to get their family members out of trouble.

Conversely, when we are purposeful about maintaining healthy family dynamics, we honor the legacy of our fore-parents. In which case, they have more time to bestow blessings upon us and fill us with wisdom. This way, we can honor our ancestors by simply spending quality time with our living loved ones and contributing to the overall advancement of our bloodline.

There is no specific method for sustaining or improving healthy family dynamics. However, there are many valuable resources for doing so if you need help in this area. Life coaches, counselors, therapists, self-help books, etc., can provide you with a wealth of knowledge on restoring and maintaining salient relationships within your family unit.

Maintaining Good Character

Good character is at the core of our destiny. The purpose of our entire journey in this realm is to develop and maintain spiritual, physical, emotional, and mental integrity. Integrity embodies the attributes of honesty and moral uprightness. I am not referring to good character or integrity from a religious perspective, though many religious systems do an excellent job integrating and implementing such teachings. Many of us learned about morality through religious systems such as Christianity and Islam. These religious systems are excellent taskmasters in that regard.

However, good character goes beyond action or inaction based on a code of moral standards established or perpetuated through a religious system. Good character is seated at the core of our being. If our mental, emotional, and spiritual faculties are aptly functional, we intuitively know right from wrong. Contrarily, many moral codes are ingrained into us through societal standards. They are not necessarily universal or God-given laws. And, they don't always apply to us on an individual level.

The basis of good character is upright thoughts, words, and actions derived from the purest intentions. In essence, our desire to exercise integrity should stem from an internal sense of morality or accomplishment rather than from fear or pressure. Good character drives us to want to do good for the sake of our personal growth and development. For this reason, character development can look different for each individual.

So, how do we determine right versus wrong? We glean this intuitive knowledge from our ancestors and spiritual team. In life, there are few absolutes. What is helpful for one person may not be beneficial to another person in terms of character development.

Even the Bible tells us that there is a season for everything under the sun (Ecclesiastes 3:2-8):

> *A time to be born and a time to die, a time to plant and a time to uproot, a time to kill and a time to heal, a time to tear down and a time to build, a time to weep and a time to laugh, a time to mourn and a time to dance, a time to scatter stones and a time to gather them, a time to embrace and a time to refrain from embracing, a time to search and a time to give up, a time to keep and a time to throw away, a*

time to tear and a time to mend, a time to be silent and a time to speak, a time to love and a time to hate, a time for war and a time for peace.

This scriptural passage indicates that we need to align with Divine timing for every action or inaction that we consider. Conversely, it does not command us to follow a prescribed set of universal rules and laws. The sum of good character is ultimately staying in alignment with our destiny. We need to move when Spirit tells us to move and stand still when Spirit indicates otherwise.

Honoring our ancestors through good character is about acting according to the intuitive knowledge that we receive from them and our spirit guides. To do so, we must be appropriately aligned with our ancestors to get clear messages from them. Many of the activities that I discussed in this chapter are helpful for this purpose. I also discuss other methods for getting clearer messages from ancestral spirits in a later chapter.

Taking Proper Care of Yourself

In order to continue your ancestral legacy, you need to take proper care of your health. When you are well, you can take much better care of your needs and your family's needs. Good hygiene and maintenance give you the capacity to improve the overall health and sustainability of your progeny and your lineage.

By taking care of yourself, you are honoring the legacy and continuity of your ancestors. When you get adequate nourishment, exercise, sleep, and rest, you are doing beneficial things for your overall health. Likewise, when you minimize the consumption of poisonous substances such as alcohol, drugs, cigarettes, processed foods, and toxic people, places, things, and ideas, you are better able to cope and function.

In which case, you are providing a stronger foundation that allows you and your family to grow and prosper. That is not to say that your life will be without challenges or troubles if you do these things. However, taking good care of yourself better equips you to manage challenges and hardships. It also helps you attract positive energy into your life and easily dispel negative energy from your environment.

Living an Authentic Life

You can likewise honor your ancestors by living an authentic life. Authenticity means living the life that you were meant to live and not comparing yourself to others. Similarly, it challenges you to live life according to your own rules and not the standards or expectations of other people. Our journey is not about pleasing or measuring up to other people.

We were all put on this earth to achieve a specific destiny. Even though our soul mission may be similar to others in specific ways, none of us have the exact same life purpose. And no two people go about accomplishing their destiny in the same manner. Therefore, it is fruitless and inauthentic to try to do so.

Even more, trying to be like someone else only delays the process of fulfilling your own destiny. In fact, doing so can even prevent you from accomplishing your purpose. As such, we must live authentic lives to perpetuate past, present, and future generations. It pleases our ancestors when we embrace our individuality and uniqueness because doing helps us advance and grow much quicker. It also makes their job a lot easier.

Fulfilling Our Ancestor's Legacy

Many of our ancestors did not have the opportunity to fulfill their lifelong goals and dreams. Notably, this applies to individuals throughout the African diaspora who have ancestors who were robbed of their basic human dignity. They often had to hide who they were or what they believed. Sadly, this has left current and future generations with a significant cultural and socioeconomic deficit.

Fortunately, many of us now have the opportunity to fulfill our dreams and live authentically. But this still doesn't negate the fact that many of our ancestors' dreams were lost and stolen. Many of them are still longing to see their desires come to fruition. As such, they often place these desires in us through biogenetic inheritance, which explains why we have particular desires that sometimes can't be easily understood.

For instance, you may all of a sudden experience the desire to take a cruise to Alaska. However, you don't have a genuine interest in this region of the world, and you may not even like sea travel. But there is this nagging feeling that you just need to get there by ship.

It could be that your great grandfather was from Alaska, and he may have been a seaman. He may have died at sea trying to get back home to your grandmother, who was anxiously waiting for him. Since he never made that trip back home to settle his affairs properly, he may be trying to use you to take this one last voyage for him. It may be that you need to give him a proper burial ceremony in his homeland. Or, it could be that you need to gain access to his estate to restore it to your family. Once you take the voyage, these things and more may be revealed to you so that you can honor his legacy.

African Spiritual Systems

This section specifically addresses individuals throughout the African diaspora. However, anyone interested in African spirituality can benefit from engaging in one of the many African-derived spiritual practices throughout the world. Don't allow your physical traits, race, or ethnic background to deter you from practicing within an African spiritual system if this is something that resonates with you. Regardless of your phenotype, you may have African ancestry, and your ancestors could be calling you back to your spiritual heritage.

Ancestor veneration is foundational to African Spirituality. If you practice one, you will eventually become acquainted with the other as the two go hand-in-hand. When you start to honor your ancestors, they will most likely help you find your way back to the spiritual system of your ancestral lineage (if you aren't already familiar with it).

But keep in mind, it is not necessary to practice African spirituality to reap the many benefits that ancestor veneration offers. In fact, numerous people of non-African descent honor their ancestors and don't subscribe to a traditional African belief system. Yet, they still receive the results they desire from this practice. However, people throughout the African diaspora tend to experience greater results when they blend ancestor veneration with the traditional spiritual systems of their lineage.

While you can communicate with your ancestors regardless of your belief system, African-derived spiritual systems can bring you into direct contact with your ancestors through divination, rituals, and ceremonies. You don't have to be an active practitioner of an African-derived spiritual system to seek the assistance of a diviner or perform sacred rites associated with these systems. However, it is more beneficial if you actively practice within one of these systems as a means of developing a deeper connection with your ancestors and the rest of your spiritual team.

I personally practice Ifa and Haitian Vodou as these systems are part of my ancestral heritage. Both of these systems have been instrumental in helping me develop a stronger connection with my ancestors. Many other African spiritual systems, including Hoodoo, Gullah Geechee, Louisiana Voodoo, Benin Vodu, Candomblé, Lucumi, Santeria, 21 Divisions, Obeah, etc., may be beneficial to you for the same purpose.

Many traditional systems still practiced today in Africa, America, the Caribbean Islands, Polynesia, Southeast Asia, etc., are ancestral-based spiritual practices. And people throughout the African diaspora still have contact with these practices that are common to their geographical region. There is a strong possibility that your ancestors likewise practiced one or more of these systems before or during colonization and slavery.

You need to do your homework if you wish for your journey into African spirituality to be successful. Take the time to learn about the system that interests you, whether you intend to simply get a reading or become a serious devotee or full initiate. Understanding the system better prepares you for the results that you can expect. You should also seek out a legitimate priest or priestess who can perform divination for you as you do your research. Divination can help you receive concrete and direct messages from your ancestors.

But it is also best to develop a relationship with your ancestors before working with an African spiritual system. Your ancestors are your first line of defense in helping you find the right system and the right diviner or spiritualist. Ask them for guidance and direction along your journey. Skipping this step can lead you down the wrong path. Though working with them in this process can be greatly rewarding on many levels.

Chapter 4: How Your Ancestors Connect with You

One question often asked about ancestor veneration is, "how do we know when our ancestors are speaking to us?" The first thing that we must understand about connecting with our ancestors is that they are constantly communicating with us in some way. However, we may not recognize it easily. Through societal conditioning, we have been compelled to believe that ancestor communication only manifests in the form of a ghostly vision or apparition.

While this can happen, it is not always the case. Generally, ancestral communication is quiet and subtle. It is founded on the awareness that our ancestors are ever-present. They are always guiding our paths whether we are aware of their existence or not. Also, we have to keep in mind that spirits communicate with us according to our needs, not our desires. They won't always show up as ghosts or apparitions - in most cases, they don't. Unless you have a specific gifting to see spirits, you may never see your ancestors in physical form.

Spiritual beings are not meant to have constant interaction in the material world. Their presence will rarely be made apparent or noticeable. There are rare occasions that we will experience their physical presence because, in most instances, we don't need to.

Their goal or purpose is not to scare us or to be a constant interruption in our lives.

However, certain emergency situations may necessitate that they make their presence apparent. For instance, if you are in immediate danger, they may appear in physical form so that you are fully aware of the message they are trying to convey. They may need to do this to startle you or get your attention so that you can quickly get out of harm's way. Other times they may be visible is when you have a substantial, high-level assignment to complete. For instance, you may need to break a generation curse, perform a ceremony for a deity, etc., that requires elevated support from them.

Otherwise, our ancestors tend to speak to us in soft and sometimes indirect ways. Their communication tends to be very gentle and non-invasive. However, if we are paying attention, we can ascertain vital knowledge that we need to live a destiny-driven life.

This chapter outlines the myriad of ways that our ancestors can and do communicate with us. Understand that their methods of communication may be different for each individual. Additionally, their approach may change over time or on certain occasions. So don't be alarmed, confused, or upset if you don't receive ancestral communication, in the same way, all the time, or in the same way as others. If you have an urgent or desperate need to feel their presence, they will manifest as needed. Simply be patient and diligent in the practice of ancestral veneration. You will indeed receive your reward for doing so.

Dreams

Dreams are the hallmark of ancestral communication in African and other traditional spiritual systems. People throughout the African diaspora have traditionally held dreams in high regard for this reason. Our ancestors and other spiritual beings speak to us when we are in a dream state, as this is when we are between the physical and spiritual worlds. This space is often referred to as the astral realm. During this state, we are more receptive to messages from our spiritual guides because we are not distracted by mundane events and happenings.

Our ancestors can give us answers to our questions, teach us how to do things, tell us about future events, or otherwise communicate messages to us through our dreams. This is why we need to pay attention to our dreams. It is especially important to observe recurring or thematic dreams. Such dreams indicate that our ancestors are trying to share vital information with us. It is likewise essential to take note of dreams that alarm or disturb us in any way. Such dreams often serve as warnings of impending events or circumstances that could adversely impact us.

Some people engage in dreamwork in order to enhance the potential, potency, and recall of their dreams. Dreamwork can include recording dreams, candle rituals, meditation, visualization, etc. These tools may be used alone or in combination with each other. I encourage you to do more research on any of these methods that are of interest to you. While I discuss these tools in other sections, I do not detail the full range of usage for each of them as that information is not within the scope of this book.

Recording your dreams is a simple practice that can help you better recall and understand the spiritual downloads you receive when you sleep. This process involves keeping a journal, notebook, or audio recorder near your bed. Upon waking, you will use these tools to chronicle everything you remember about your dreams. This process is effectively a mind dump whereby you simply write what you remember without initially judging or interpreting the information.

The most important part of this process is to record as much detail about the dream as possible. Once you write what you remember, you can go back and catalog more details. Some common writing prompts for dream recall include:

- How did it make you feel while you were sleeping? Upon waking?
- Did you notice anything that stood out or seemed out of place?

- Did the dream seem real?

Your feelings during or after the dream can give you a good indication regarding its overall message or tone. If you felt good, uplifted, or joyful, chances are the message was meant to bring good tidings. Likewise, if you experienced distress, anxiety, nervousness, or fear, the message was most likely meant to be a warning. If you noticed something in particular that deeply resonated with you about the dream, you should pay close attention to it. This information usually gives you vital clues regarding the main message of the dream.

If your dream seemed real or tangible, it was most likely a message sent from your ancestors. But, keep in mind dreams do not always play out the exact same way in real life. Oftentimes, they serve as metaphors or parables that present us with signs of upcoming events or answers to questions. For example, if you dreamed about a baby and you felt excited or happy, this may indicate a rebirth or renewal period for you or a situation in your life. It may not foretell a literal pregnancy for you or someone else.

Once you have outlined the details, record your dream interpretation (if you have one). Write down what you thought the dream meant in your own words. You don't have to do this right away. Actually, it may be best to take some time to process the dream before trying to interpret it. You may need hours, days, weeks, or even months to work out a functional interpretation - do it at your own pace.

If you can't construct an amenable dream interpretation, you may want to consult a dream interpretation guide or specialist. I usually consult my Oluwo (Ifa priest) whenever I have a disturbing dream that I can't easily understand. Sometimes, these dreams indicate that spiritual intervention is required to maintain peace, harmony, and balance in my life.

There are also plenty of online articles and posts, books, seminars, practitioners, etc., that can assist you in this area. But be careful when engaging with such resources as dreams are highly subjective. While there are universal themes in dreams, the meaning of your dreams often directly correlates with the circumstances of your life.

Journaling

Another effective dreamwork method involves journaling, whereby you write a question in a notebook before you fall asleep. You can also ask the question to your ancestors before or after writing it in your journal or notebook. When you wake, you should complete the same recording process as outlined in the previous section. Then, determine if the elements of your dream correspond to the question(s) that you asked.

It may not be immediately apparent what your dream meant, but you can and should revisit your recordings from time to time. Doing so will help you determine if there are any patterns in the manifestation of your dreams. The more you engage in this practice, the better you will become at interpreting your dreams. You will also become more familiar with your ancestors' communication style as you record and review your dreams.

Candle Work

Candle rituals or candle magic also serve the purpose of potentiating dreams. As discussed previously, candles are spiritual conduits. Therefore, initiating candle work before going to sleep can significantly enhance the possibility of dreaming. There are several ways to conduct candle rituals for this purpose. Some methods are more complex than others, and some are connected with specific spiritual systems. For the sake of simplicity, I have outlined an easy candle ritual that can be performed by anyone who practices within any spiritual system.

To complete this ritual, you will need a white candle, lighter (or match), and glass of water. Candles encased in jars have a protective barrier that is helpful when doing candle work around young children or animals. However, you can use a loose candle and place it in enamelware, glass, or another fireproof container. Once you have obtained the candle for your ritual, cleanse it with a spiritual perfume like Florida or rose water before lighting it. This process helps clear the candle of unpleasant or undesirable energies that may be attached to it.

After cleansing the candle, hold it in your hand and consecrate or devote it to your ancestors. Speaking a statement signifying that you are dedicating the candle to your ancestors is sufficient for this purpose. After that, tell your ancestors why you are lighting the candle. If you have a specific question or inquiry for them, you can ask it and request that they answer it through your dreams.

Next, place the candle on a table or solid service near your bed and light it. Put the glass of water next to the candle. The water should be in a clear glass container or enamelware mug - avoid using plastic containers or other synthetic materials when doing spiritual work. These types of materials can attract unclean energies and are generally considered disrespectful when honoring any kind of spirit.

After finalizing the ritual, you can lay down and sleep. If you are uncomfortable with allowing the candle to burn while you sleep, let it burn for about an hour before falling asleep. Then, blow the candle out and leave it next to your bed while you sleep. You can discard the candle or reuse it for the same purpose at a different time upon waking. This ritual can be done daily, weekly, monthly, or at other intervals that suit your schedule and lifestyle.

It is best not to sleep in the bed with anyone when doing candle work of this type. If it is not possible to sleep in the bed alone, sleep on the floor, on the sofa, or in another area where you can be by yourself. Sleeping alone prevents you from mixing the energy of someone else with your essence. It provides a clear channel for the flow of communication between you and your ancestors.

Meditation and Visualization

Meditation, visualization, or any other mind-clearing activities are also beneficial for dream potentiation and recall. The more you work with these practices, the more you enhance your ability to dream and easily recall your dreams. These methods are addressed in more detail in the next chapter.

Apparitions

Ancestors can and sometimes do manifest in physical form as ghosts or apparitions. However, this is not a common phenomenon that the average person experiences. If your ancestors manifest as apparitions, they usually do so because they have a critical message to relay to you. Generally, such messages are urgent, as mentioned previously.

For instance, if you are about to get robbed, injured, or otherwise harmed in some way, your ancestors may appear in physical form to quickly get your attention. They may also manifest in this form to startle or frighten an individual who is about to harm you. Additionally, your ancestors may manifest in physical form to provide comfort to you in a time of need. Ghostly appearances may occur if you are experiencing significant grief or other emotions that may have a profound impact on your well-being. Your ancestors may also appear to you if you request their presence. However, this is not always guaranteed.

Again, spirits belong in the astral realm, just as humans belong in the earthly realm. While there are other reasons you may have ghostly encounters, this is not the norm. Many people expect to immediately see apparitions when they connect with their ancestors because of media hype that perpetuates spiritual phenomena as ghostly or otherworldly experiences. But this does not occur as frequently or as freakily as the movies sometimes depict.

Ancestral spirits do not desire to scare or frighten us. They want to have a loving, close relationship with us. They understand that scare tactics are not the way to achieve this goal. If you have scary or unnerving encounters with ghosts on a regular basis, this is generally not considered to be positive or conducive to your well-being. You may be encountering lower-level or earthbound spirits. In which case, it is best to remove such entities from your space. A spiritualist can often assist you if these types of manifestations are causing issues in your life.

There are special circumstances in which you may frequently encounter ghosts or apparitions. But again, such encounters should not be spooky or frightening. These circumstances generally involve someone like a shaman, oracle, or clairvoyant who has the gift of communicating with spirits. In these instances, the individual can see and communicate with the dead with relative ease and profound efficiency.

Inner Knowing

Our ancestors (as well as other spirits) speak to us through our intuition or inner knowing. This process is also referred to as telepathy. Sometimes we just know things. We know what to do in a specific situation, we know something about someone, we know how to do something, etc., without any previous knowledge of these things.

Our intuition is a guiding compass - it shows us how to navigate our way through life so that we may fulfill our destinies. Our ancestors play a vital role in this process. When our intuition guides our actions, we are honoring our ancestors. In turn, they reciprocate by continuing to enhance our intuitive knowledge base. Thus, our intuition grows stronger, and we become more confident in this ability.

On the other hand, the more we ignore our intuition, the weaker it becomes. It can become so debilitated that we cannot discern when our ancestors are trying to communicate with us. Your intuition must guide you because only you, your ancestors, and your spirit guides genuinely know what is best for your life.

Our intuition can also become weakened through religion. Most major religions teach the concept of following the guidelines of a master teacher, prophet, or incarnate god. The premise of these religions is centered around adhering to strict moral principles and codes of conduct. While doing so can benefit society collectively, this concept does not fully nurture us on an individual level.

Religion sometimes ignores the fact that we are all spirits connected to the Great Spirit. In which case, we all have the ability to gain knowledge of right and wrong through our inner knowing. Blindly following someone else's guidance can be gravely dangerous as it can keep us from aligning with our purpose.

Distractions also weaken our intuitive knowing. When we are constantly bombarded with external messages and communication, it isn't easy to discern when our ancestors speak to us. If we constantly check our social media accounts, watch television, or otherwise engage in distracting activities, it is more difficult to "hear ourselves think." Thereby, we miss many important messages that can help us grow and develop in healthy, sustainable ways.

Visions

Some people have visions in which they see past, present, or future events unfold. These visions typically occur when one is in a trance-like or hypnotic state. Though, they can also happen during the dream state. Such visions are often relayed to individuals by their ancestors.

During a trance, an individual is semi-conscious, which enhances their capacity to see into the spiritual realm. Their faculties are not otherwise engaged in earthly matters during this time. Thus, the individual can be fully attentive to spiritual communication. These types of visions are described in religious texts such as the Bible. In narratives about Isaiah, Ezekiel, Peter, John the Revelator, and several others, we get a glimpse of what some people have experienced during a trance. There are many more modern-day examples of this same phenomenon. In these cases, individuals express the ability to gain high-level spiritual insight that is not otherwise available to them in a normal waking state.

Trance states can be induced through meditation, hypnosis, psychedelic drugs, or other mechanisms designed to put an individual in an altered state of consciousness. However, ancestral visions are often experienced during involuntary trance-like states, which means that the individual has no control over the process. As with other forms of spiritual communication, everyone does not experience visions.

Yet, for those who do, this is an effective means of communication with the ancestral realm.

Audible Voices

Some people can hear their ancestors speak to them in an audible voice that is not apparent to others. Such feedback is often distinct and specific, though it can also be short and direct. Messages presented in this form usually don't require further clarification. And generally, there is nothing you can do to potentiate this type of feedback. Some people have an innate gift for hearing spirits in the same way that some people can see ghosts or apparitions. You can ask your ancestors or your spiritual team to speak to you in this way, but keep in mind that they are not obliged to honor your request.

Be mindful that audible ancestral feedback always serves a practical and meaningful purpose. Ancestors don't generally engage in audible communication simply for the sake of having a conversation with you. Also, they will *never* tell you to do things that are harmful to yourself or others. If you hear voices telling you to engage in harmful or dangerous activities, this is not a message from your ancestors or benevolent spirits. Always remember that good and evil spirits can communicate with us in many forms. In which case, you need to distinguish between the two when engaging with the spirit realm.

Benevolent or good spirits communicate to help us advance and grow. They don't engage in communication simply for the sake of talking, gossiping, or otherwise spreading useless or harmful information. While they may warn us about certain things, their goal is not to make us fearful, anxious, or uneasy. They are part of our spiritual army, which is a shield or safeguard designed to protect and nurture us.

Contrarily, malevolent or evil spirits do communicate with us for nefarious and sinister reasons. Therefore, if you are hearing voices or experiencing other communication that is not beneficial or practical, you need to remove these energies from your environment. As previously mentioned, spiritualists are effective for such purposes. You can also eliminate malevolent or evil spirits by removing toxic people, places, things, and ideas from your environment. Other spiritual tools such as prayers, fasts, herbs, etc., are also effective for banishing evil spirits. These tools are discussed in more detail in a later chapter.

Synchronicity

Synchronicity is when seemingly unrelated events occur at or near the same time. There are many examples of synchronistic events that can occur in your life. For instance, you could start thinking about someone you haven't seen or talked to in years, and within a few minutes, days, or weeks you may see this person or receive a call or text from them. You may even be thinking about or looking at a word or phrase, and someone says it at the exact moment or shortly thereafter. You may be questioning something, and the answer manifests itself almost instantaneously.

As with many other forms of communication I have already mentioned, experiencing synchronicities is also a form of ancestral communication. But keep in mind that other spirits can also communicate with you through synchronistic events and occurrences. Though synchronicities can occur to anyone, they tend to be universal occurrences for individuals who are experiencing a spiritual awakening.

This phenomenon is thought to be a way of the universe telling us that we are on the right track. Synchronicities also communicate direct messages to us, similar to other forms of spiritual dialogue. When we begin to experience synchronicities, we are synchronizing with the frequency of the universe. Our thoughts, words, and actions are lining up with the flow of the cosmos, which gives us greater access to spiritual wisdom and knowledge that propels us toward our destiny with immense speed and accuracy.

When we have knowledge of something before or at the same time it occurs, we are accessing ancient records from our ancestral DNA. We are able to retrieve this information because we are proving ourselves worthy of understanding and guarding the secrets of the universe. As such, synchronicities usually intensify as we grow in our spiritual walk.

Feathers

Like dreams, feathers are thought to be the language of the ancestors in many cultures throughout the world. The unusual appearance of a feather in your daily life could indicate that a loved one is trying to contact you. By unusual, I mean that a feather shows up in a place where it should typically not be. Even more important than the presence of the feather is your awareness of it. If your attention is drawn to the feather, or you feel some type of connection to it, it may be a form of spiritual communication. Such occurrences are synchronistic by their very nature.

Feathers come from birds that often have the ability to fly, which means that they can reach the heights of the heavens. Birds have long been seen as the most spiritual animals since they have the natural ability to reach heights that humans and other beings cannot achieve. This ability puts them in direct alignment with the Divine. Because of this ability, these sacred animals can effortlessly deliver messages from our ancestors and other spiritual beings.

Beyond the feather itself, its color holds significance and meaning. However, the circumstances surrounding the appearance of the feather can also give you greater detail about the message your ancestors are trying to convey. For instance, a black feather correlates with protection, warning, repelling negative energy, mystical wisdom, etc.

Let's say you are contemplating going to a party on your way to work. However, you feel unsure or uneasy about attending the party. You may be deep in thought about your decision as you walk into your office. As soon as you open the door, your attention is immediately drawn to a black feather in the corner of your office. However, you have never seen a feather in your office before. The appearance of the feather in this location at the specific time you were thinking about the party could be a warning. It may be admonishing you not to go to the party.

Feather color symbolism tends to correlate with the meaning of colors in general. Table 4-1 outlines common feather meanings based on color. You may find that these meanings vary by culture or tradition. Again, it is vital to determine your own interpretation of the feather symbology as it will be highly connected to your personal experience.

Color	Meaning or Symbolism
Black	Mysticism, death, protection, warning
Blue	Psychic awareness, spiritual awareness, peace
Brown	Grounding, stability, home, friendships
Green	Health, well-being, prosperity, success
Orange	Change, optimism, creativity, energy
Pink	Romantic love, compassion, honor, harmony
Purple	Spiritual consciousness, spiritual awakening, spiritual growth, spiritual connectedness
Red	Passion, emotions, courage, good fortune
White	Purity, cleanliness, peace, joy, hope
Yellow	Vision, cheerfulness, intellectual ability, alertness

Table 4-1: Feather Color Symbolism

Numbers

Numbers have significant meanings - some people consider numbers to be the sustenance of the universe. It is said that every structure that exists mathematically exists in the physical realm as well. So, when you experience an acute awareness of repeating numbers, your ancestors are probably trying to get your attention. Also, when you begin noticing recurring, seemingly insignificant numbers or number patterns in your daily environment, the spirit realm may be connecting with you.

Numbers are the language of our ancestors, angels, and other spirit beings. The first way you know that your ancestors are communicating with you through numbers is when you begin to notice numbers in your everyday environment. Your attention may be drawn to numbers on a clock, receipt, phone, vehicle tag, odometer, sign, billboard, fortune cookie, etc.

These numbers may begin to show up consistently in your everyday environment. Many people report seeing 11:11 repeatedly when they first become aware of numbers in their spiritual journey. However, other numbers such as 22, 33, 44, etc., are also commonly cited when people experience this phenomenon. Many people in the spiritual community consider this as a sign of the beginning of a spiritual awakening journey.

Each number or number sequence has its meaning. Most numbers are symbolically connected to various universal, cultural, and social concepts. You can determine the meaning of many base numbers and number sequences by doing an internet search or reading numerology books that include number interpretations and meanings. Generally, your research will yield an overabundance of results. Some of the number symbolisms you find will be similar, and some may be contradictory.

These types of resources can provide an excellent foundation for helping you to understand number meanings. However, you will need to interpret the number symbolism for yourself. By this, I mean that you will have to dig deeper into your circumstances to determine which interpretation is appropriate for your situation.

As always, be led by your intuition. If the meaning you discover through your research doesn't feel right to you or suit your specific circumstance, it is probably not the correct interpretation. Also, be cautious of negative or oppressive interpretations of number meanings. Suppose you find a website, person, book, or another resource that consistently represents number interpretations in a negative, demeaning, anxiety-inducing, or otherwise undesirable light. Such analyses are usually personal and not connected to universal or cultural meanings of numbers. As such, they may not be beneficial for you if they are heavily focused on one person's experience.

While numbers can be used to warn you about certain events or circumstances, your ancestors do not use numbers to cause you anxiety or stress. Numbers used to communicate warnings serve as a safeguard or protective barrier, not a threatening or disempowering device. Numbers have universal frequencies and meanings - numerical vibrations are not fear-based. Instead, they tend to have a positive vibe even when they are used to warn us about something.

You can use many tools to determine the precise meaning of numbers when they appear in your life. These tools include your thoughts, intentions, people, places, things, or other aspects of your surroundings. When you first begin to notice repetitive numbers, pay attention to what you are thinking about at the time. Usually, the number that shows up may answer a question or concern that you are trying to sort out.

For instance, you may be thinking about joining a particular spiritual or religious group. Every time you start to focus on joining this group, you notice that the number 11:11 appears. The number 11 represents the beginning of a spiritual awakening, enlightenment, inspiration, intuition, connection to our higher self, etc. Thus, this could signify that joining the group may be instrumental to your spiritual growth and development.

Again, numbers have many different meanings. So, it may take more digging to determine which interpretation resonates with you. If the meaning doesn't feel right, it is probably not the message your ancestors were trying to relay. Therefore, it is incumbent upon you to determine which meaning applies to you at any given moment. When in doubt, simply ask your ancestors to show you what they are trying to communicate. They will help you figure it out in due time.

Nature

Being out in nature is a great way to hear ancestral communication more clearly. However, your ancestors can likewise communicate with you through natural elements such as the sun and moon, water, fire, rocks, wind, clouds, flowers, birds, etc. Keep in mind that every natural element is a spirit in its own right. Thus, any facet of nature can also communicate with you without the intervention of other spiritual forces.

However, our ancestors also work in collaboration with these spiritual elements on occasion. They can bring our attention to specific natural phenomena that can give us messages. For example, you may all of a sudden notice a peculiar shape in the clouds or an oddly formed rock or tree. The formation could be the answer to your question, or it could trigger a thought that gives you the answer.

You may even hear your ancestors whisper to you through the rustling of the wind or the soft drizzle of the rain. They may use such tools to deliver messages of transformation, transition, change, or cleansing. There are many ways that our ancestors can and do interact with us through nature. This topic is discussed in more detail in a later chapter.

Music

As discussed earlier, music can play a vital role in your connection with your ancestors. You can use music as a conduit to wake your ancestors up or invite them into your sacred space. You can also use music to get you in the right vibe to receive ancestral messages, which is also outlined in greater depth in a later chapter.

However, this section focuses on how ancestral spirits can and do communicate through music. Ancestors can speak with you through music in a number of different ways. They can use a song or beat to connect you to someone or something, they can use lyrics to convey important messages, or they can use music to rouse or wake you up.

Sometimes music serves as a connection tool. You may start to hear a specific song in various, unrelated environments. The tune could be something you have never heard before, or it could be very familiar to you. It may remind you of one of your lost loved ones, a living person, or even an inanimate object. Your ancestors could be trying to remind you of their presence, make you aware of a person or situation, or give you the answer to a question that you have. In particular, if the song reminds you of a specific ancestor, this could signify that that particular ancestor is working with you.

Your ancestors can also directly answer your questions or simply relay information to you through song lyrics. You may hear specific verses when thinking about something or someone. If you become acutely aware of what the singer is saying and the message resonates with you on a deep level, your ancestors may be trying to communicate with you.

For instance, you may be wondering if one of your lost loved ones is okay. Let's say that the loved one's name is Sara. You may begin to hear a song or songs with the name Sara in the lyrics almost everywhere you go. Every time you hear these lyrics, you feel happy and at peace. This is a strong indication that Sara is showing you that she is well and in a good place.

This example is one way your ancestors can speak to you through song lyrics. Many people have these types of synchronistic experiences with music on a regular basis. If you experience such phenomena, pay attention to your thoughts or environment as they can give you important indicators about the message your ancestors are trying to relay to you.

Ancestors also use music to rouse our spirits. You may be in a depressed mood or otherwise vibrating on a low frequency. You could be feeling so sorry for yourself to the point that you are ready to give up on something, someone, or life itself. Otherwise, you might simply be feeling lethargic about completing a Divine task or duty that you have been called to do. In these instances, ancestral spirits can activate music in your environment to uplift your mood.

You may start hearing inspirational music in the background that reminds you that you have a reason to keep going. The lyrics may remind you of your destiny and why you are a vital part of society, or the song may remind you of the human condition and that you are not alone in your plight. On the other hand, the music may merely shift your energy and inspire you to have uplifting thoughts. Regardless of the reason, our ancestors often use music to rouse us from our slumber and get us going in the right direction.

As a side note, similar occurrences can happen through movies, videos, or any other types of media. Remember that our ancestors are energy, so they are strongly connected to vibrational conduits such as these. They can use many different platforms for the same purpose.

Animals

Ancestors and animals often have a symbiotic relationship since animals are also forces of nature, as discussed in the previous section. Animals can work with our ancestors to communicate messages to us. Sometimes our ancestors place certain animals in our paths or make us aware of animals along our path as messenger guides. In this way, our ancestors sometimes use animals to connect with us.

Animal messengers can appear in real life, dreams, or visions. Their unexpected or mysterious presence at specific times or in certain places is often an indication of communication from the spirit realm. If an animal seems out of place in a particular environment or if you become acutely aware of an animal in its native habitat, this usually indicates that the animal is transmitting some type of message to you.

An incident that I experienced years ago when I lived in the Middle East serves as a personal example of animal communication from my ancestors. This event occurred at the beginning of a significant juncture in my spiritual awakening journey. At that time, I started experiencing many signs and wonders from my ancestors who were on a mission to get my attention. I was already aware of the importance of synchronicities, numerology, and other forms of ancestral communication. I was also beginning to receive animal messages, so I was aware of the significance of their presence. This knowledge made me acutely aware of the appearance of a rabbit that I saw one morning as I was leaving my compound for work.

My family was visiting the U.S. at that time, so I was alone. I lived in a very active community where children and housewives were usually outside in the morning. But on that particular day, no one was outside when I left for work, which was very odd. As I left my apartment and locked my door, I turned around and noticed a white rabbit hopping across the concrete pavement that lined my neighbor's walkway. This siting was very odd because white rabbits are not common or indigenous to the geographical region where I lived.

Undoubtedly the rabbit captured my full attention, so I decided to record it. I probably spent about 15-20 minutes watching and recording the rabbit. No one came outside, so I was the only one who saw the rabbit during that particular moment. After I finished the recording, I left for work and meditated on the incident as I drove. I knew that my ancestors were communicating with me because they had placed animal messengers in my path in the previous months. So, I had become adept at interpreting animal symbology.

When I reached my office, I looked up the meaning of white rabbits and discovered that they represent rapid change, fertility, prosperity, and abundance, among other things. This message was so timely as I was very confused and frustrated about many things during that period of my life. As I mentioned, I was undergoing a major phase of my spiritual awakening process. It was quite daunting for me, so this message was very encouraging. It was also very accurate.

Less than three months after seeing the rabbit, my family and I began making plans to move back to the U.S. About three months later, we were back home. Soon after, I experienced a great deal of progress in my spiritual journey, which also impacted my physical well-being. I realized that I needed to be in the U.S.

for my spiritual journey to progress in the way it did. The rabbit was definitely an omen of blessings and prosperity for me, which I needed at that time in my life. The message it delivered was encouraging as it helped me push through a rough patch in my spiritual journey.

Sometimes an animal messenger will only appear once in certain instances, like in the example I described. If you get the message the first time, there is usually no need for the animal to appear in the same capacity again. However, repeatedly seeing the same animal or animal species in various contexts is a strong indicator that your spiritual team is trying to get your attention.

Animal messages tend to be very direct and concrete in their foundational meaning. Many cultures throughout the world have long-established traditions related to the significance of the appearance of certain animals. However, cultural interpretations of animal symbology can vary quite extensively. Animal messages are often decoded based on how and when the animal appears in your environment. The particular type and color of the animal are also taken into consideration. Therefore, I recommend using an interpretation most closely related to your heritage when deciphering animal messages.

As always, it is best to check your thoughts or intentions when your ancestors send an animal messenger along your path. Incorporating your intuition will give you the best clues about the message being conveyed. Likewise, a spiritualist who specializes in animal symbology may be able to interpret the meaning of animal messages for you. There are also numerous books, articles, guides, etc., that may help you uncover the meaning of animal messages.

Young Children

Ancestral spirits often communicate with young children because of their youth and innocence. Young children are perceptive to the spiritual realm because they recently left this space prior to their incarnation into the earthly realm. They usually have a strong connection with ancestral and other spirits for this very reason.

Additionally, young children are still innocent and naive to the indoctrination of adults. They still believe in fairies, elms, pixies, unicorns, etc., because they often have fluid communication with these beings. These spiritual forces are very much so part of our reality. Though, they are referenced by different names in various cultures throughout the world. Also, popular culture has relegated them to cartoon status, which has misconstrued the true nature of these spirit beings.

Metaphysical communication is part of children's daily reality because they interact with such beings on a regular basis. Likewise, children communicate with lost loved ones who have passed to the spiritual realm. Ancestors sometimes manifest in the form of an imaginary friend that a child may have during their early years. A child can interact for hours with such an invisible being. At the same time, the child is usually learning valuable lessons and relaying messages sent by our lost loved ones during these interactions.

The average adult may dismiss such a notion of an imaginary friend as child's play. But children are often communing with ancestors or other spirit beings. Such exchanges are evident when a child relays uncanny messages that they could not have known before. For instance, the child may tell you vivid and accurate details about a lost loved one they have never met before. The child may give you names, addresses, phone numbers, physical descriptions, historical information, secrets, etc., that they receive from the spiritual realm. In which case, the child could be interacting with an ancestral spirit.

Ancestors are able to transmit very valuable information through young children. In particular, verbal children can relay direct messages in real-time. So, pay attention when children in your environment are speaking. Even if they appear to be speaking gibberish, they may be giving you an important message.

However, a strong word of caution must be given in this section. Just as good and benevolent beings can interact with young children, evil or malevolent spirits can likewise do so. If you think a child is interacting with ancestral or other spirits, and the child appears frightened, disturbed, or upset in any way, you should investigate more.

A malicious or malevolent spirit may be interacting with the child if they seem uneasy, anxious, scared, fearful, depressed, or otherwise exhibit negative signs and symptoms. In which case, it is best to consult a spiritualist if you are not experienced with banishing evil entities. If you are skilled in this area, you can employ techniques that you are familiar with to dispel the evil energies. Either way, you should remove such spirits from the child's environment as soon as possible.

Fragrances and Scents

If you mysteriously smell a fragrance or scent associated with a deceased loved one, chances are the essence of that individual is in your midst. People commonly report having such encounters years after the death of their loved ones in spaces that should otherwise be devoid of such smells. Also, other scents such as soaps, deodorants, food aromas, pipe or cigarette smoke, etc. sometimes present in the same manner.

The key to determining if the scent is from an ancestor is based on how it manifests. It is not uncommon to smell the cologne or perfume of a lost loved one in public spaces when surrounded by other people. After all, many people often use the same body fragrances. It is also not unusual to smell such scents when they have been deliberately sprayed or projected in the environment by someone else.

For instance, your sister may decide to cook grandma's favorite biscuit recipe while staying at your home over the weekend. You are not aware that she is in the kitchen cooking since you are still in bed. As the smell of the cooking biscuits begins to fill your home, you will probably start to think about your deceased grandmother.

However, the old, familiar aroma of your grandma's biscuits is emanating from a tangible, physical force in this instance. This doesn't mean that your grandma's essence isn't present at the time. In fact, she could have inspired your sister to cook the biscuits that morning. But because there was a direct and clear physical connection to the smell, it cannot be conclusively labeled as an ancestral encounter.

On the other hand, smells and scents that emanate from the spiritual realm do not have a discernable physical source. They seemingly manifest out of nowhere and often disappear within a short span of time. Such scents can be emitted while one is in a wakeful or sleep state. However, it is common that only one or a few people will detect these scents.

These types of experiences are quite often ancestral encounters.

They can be indicators that your ancestors are present. Our ancestors commonly use fragrances as a subtle form of communication because it is usually not meant to relay a direct message. Instead, our ancestors use familiar scents and fragrances to make us aware of their loving and attentive presence.

Electrical Interferences

Constant or abnormal electrical interferences may also signal that your ancestors are trying to communicate with you. Spirits are energy, so when they come in contact with electricity, odd things can start happening. Their presence may cause lights to blink or switch on or off without physical intervention or similar interferences. If benevolent spirits are the cause of such activity, they usually have an attention-getting agenda. Their goal may be to make you aware of their presence for various reasons.

If you experience such activity, it is a good idea to begin doing ancestral veneration work. This way, you can direct or guide the energy in the proper direction. Likewise, you can better position yourself to hear from and understand the spirits. Chances are, once you receive the message they were trying to relay, the activity will stop.

But, keep in mind that mischievous spirits are also capable of interfering with electrical circuits. Thus, another type of energy may be at play, and its motives may not be so benevolent. The easiest way to know the difference is to do energy clearing work and start honoring your ancestors. If the activity continues, you may need help from someone experienced with removing evil spirits.

Even if mischievous spirits caused the interferences, you should still engage in an ancestral veneration practice after clearing the energies. It is always beneficial to maintain a close relationship with your ancestors. They are your first line of defense against such disruptions. The previous chapter discussed many things that you can do to honor your ancestors. Either of these methods can help you establish a connection with your ancestors.

Hot or Cold Sensations

If you start feeling hot or cold touchpoints in different regions of your body, an ancestral spirit may be with you. However, you should first check to determine if there is a physiological reason related to these sensations. If you are experiencing such symptoms and they are causing you pain or discomfort, you should seek the advice of a qualified healthcare professional as soon as possible. These could be symptoms of a serious medical condition, so exercise caution and wisdom before making assumptions.

Otherwise, if the feelings are harmless and do not cause you mental or physical discomfort, it could indicate that your ancestors are connecting with you. If you feel frightened, startled, fearful, or otherwise uncomfortable when these sensations occur, mischievous spirits are possibly in your environment. In which case, you need to remove them as discussed in previous sections.

The most important thing to do is check your emotional state when you experience such phenomena. First, determine how you feel. Then, assess what is going on in your life and environment at the time. Our ancestors generally allow us to sense such vibrations when they are trying to comfort us. They want us to know that we are not alone in our experience.

Misplaced or Missing Objects

Another attention-getting activity that ancestors sometimes engage in is moving or misplacing objects. Again, this activity is usually done to make you acutely aware of their presence. Typically, ancestors move your things around when you are out of alignment with them.

Similar to electrical interferences, this is nothing to worry about as long as the behavior is benign and not related to a health condition. If you are consistently misplacing objects, you could be experiencing memory problems indicative of dementia or related conditions. Therefore, it is prudent to consult with a qualified healthcare professional to determine if you have an underlying illness. If this is not the case, ask your ancestors what message they want to relay to you. If they are the source of the issue, they will soon reveal their reasons.

Answered Requests and Petitions

One of the easiest and probably best ways to know that your ancestors are communicating with you is through answered prayer requests. If you ask your ancestors for something and receive it, you know that they have heard and responded to you. Answered prayers are a point-blank, straightforward way that our ancestors communicate with us.

To keep track of your requests, write them in a journal. Every time you ask your ancestors for something, write your prayer down along with the date and time of the request. Thereafter, record the date and time or timeframe when they responded to your request. Journaling will help you keep track of when and how your ancestors reply to you.

Always be specific when asking your ancestors for help. For example, if you need a vehicle, don't just ask for any type of automobile. Ask for a vehicle that will suit your highest and greatest good. Ultimately, you want a reliable mode of transportation. You can also ask for a specific make, model, color, features, etc. However, keep in mind that what you desire may not be in your best interest.

Therefore, it is always good to ask for things that will serve you in the best possible way. Our ancestors know our needs better than we do, in most instances. Sometimes we have desires that aren't necessarily the best option for us. For example, you may want an expensive vehicle with all the trimmings, but it may not be aligned with your budget.

Also, note that prayer combined with proper veneration is more effective for getting faster results to your requests. Our ancestors were once human and are fully aware of human nature. They do not want you to use them like a genie in a bottle. In most cases, they won't even allow you to do so. Therefore, you should have a proper veneration practice established before you start asking for things.

The spirit realm operates from the premise of reciprocity. You have to give something in order to get something. Nothing in the spirit realm is free. We give offerings to our ancestors as a way of feeding their energy. This process also helps us connect with them and our needs and desires on a deeper level.

Additionally, giving in exchange for getting gives you a greater appreciation for what you receive. When you work for something, you tend to cherish and nurture it in a different way than when you get it for free.

You should likewise operate in honesty and integrity when implementing this practice. Your ancestors can easily spot inauthenticity. Thus, the primary purpose of your practice should be to honor your ancestors rather than only receiving favors from them. Spend time being grateful for the blessings that they give you. I recommend keeping a gratitude journal for this purpose. Also, whisper prayers of thanksgiving immediately upon receiving answered prayer requests.

Illnesses or Diseases

The last three forms of ancestral communication discussed in this chapter are not as pleasurable as the previously discussed types. Instead, they are generally last-ditch efforts when your ancestors have failed to get your attention through other means. When your ancestors are relegated to using extreme measures to get your attention, the message is critical. Therefore, it is imperative to heed the call of your ancestors when they reach out to you in more amicable ways.

As I write about the following types of ancestral communication, I am reminded of the Black Panther (2018) movie line when the character N'Jobu stated, "they won't knock again." This was in reference to his brother, the King of Wakanda, entering his apartment with his two supernatural female warrior soldiers. In this scene, N'Jobu was letting his friend know that if he didn't open the door the first time, their next attempt to get into the apartment would not be so pleasant. Ancestral communication follows a similarly progressive pattern. When we don't heed our ancestor's initial attempts to get our attention, we leave them with no choice but to employ harsher measures. Serious illnesses and diseases are an example of this type of communication. Ancestors may cause you to be ill for a certain period to rouse you to a wakeful state. But keep in mind that ancestor-imposed illnesses should not be confused with physical or behavioral health conditions that can typically be resolved by traditional or allopathic medicine.

The distinguishing factor in these types of illnesses is that they are unresponsive to such treatment modalities. Even more, doctors usually can't find a root or underlying cause for the disease or condition. Tests and other diagnostic results may consistently present as normal or without significant cause for concern.

If you or someone in your family is experiencing such a situation, it could be a sign that your ancestors are trying to get your attention. The only sure-fire way to know is to make contact with the ancestral realm. You can do this yourself using some of the techniques that I described in the previous chapter. However, a diviner is the most helpful resource for determining the legitimacy of an ancestor-induced illness. In ancestral-based spiritual systems such as Vodou, Lucumi, Santeria, Obeah, Shamanism, and the like, a priest or priestess can contact the spirit realm to determine the underlying source of the health problem.

If your ancestors caused your illness, your condition will improve once you implement the remedy they prescribed through the divination process. Sometimes, the prescription is a ritual or ceremony designed to reconcile your connection with your ancestors. Other times it may be an herbal potion to alleviate the malady. The remedy could likewise involve behavioral changes that can help you better align with your destiny. As with allopathic medicine, the cure is based on the underlying cause, and the ultimate goal is to restore you or your family member to wholeness. Once your health is restored, you need to maintain a clear line of communication with your ancestors to prevent similar or worse issues in the future.

Significant Problems or Challenges

Similar to causing diseases and illnesses, ancestors can wreak havoc in other areas of your life as well. They can stir up turbulence that can impact your spiritual, financial, and social well-being. Some common examples of issues or problems that ancestors can cause, perpetuate, or allow in your life include the following:

- Poverty, unemployment, under-employment, lack of socio-economic progress
- Broken families, divorce, domestic discord, single parenthood, inability to get married

111

- Self-esteem issues, lack of confidence, arrogance, vanity, narcissism, jealousy, envy, competitiveness
- Suicide, homicide, abuse, and other acts of violence
- Homelessness, vagabonding, residential instability, imprisonment, recidivism
- Sex addiction, promiscuity, infidelity, incest, molestation, and all other forms of sexual immorality
- Spiritual and ritual abuse, spiritual confusion, consistently being subjected to witchcraft, black magic, or spiritual attacks

These types of problems often manifest as generational curses or patterns. The same is true for diseases or illnesses. These types of afflictions tend to have far-reaching effects for many generations in a particular bloodline. In which case, such maladies indicate a severe breach in your ancestral connection that should be reconciled as soon as possible.

An example of this is a family lineage that has suffered from extreme poverty for several generations. Poverty is a special kind of curse because it affects every aspect of a person's life. It is a form of severe bondage that has the propensity to keep one from fulfilling their destiny, which is the underlying goal of poverty. Sadly, many people throughout the African diaspora suffer from this curse, which has inhibited our global advancement. Much of this has to do with us leaving our ancestral heritage, culture, and spirituality. Consequently, we have yielded our power in the process.

However, all is not lost. Ancestor veneration can help you determine the origin of such challenges. If your ancestors have caused these issues or if they have other spiritual roots, you can find a remedy by consulting with a qualified diviner. Doing so has worked for many of my clients who experienced significant problems due to generational curses. They overcame these adverse patterns with remedies that they received through divination and a consistent ancestral veneration practice.

Near-Death Experiences

A near-death experience could indicate that you are heading down a dangerous path that could lead to permanent death in a specific area of your life. Your ancestors may allow you to have such experiences to keep you out of trouble in the long run. For instance, you may be involved in an abusive relationship, criminal activity, or otherwise engaged in dangerous behavioral patterns. Your ancestors may allow you to come in close contact with death to show you that you are on the brink of self-destruction.

Your behavior may be leading you down the road to imprisonment, serious health problems, divorce, financial ruin, etc. By initiating a near-death experience, your ancestors are warning you to stop the behavior before it is too late. The near-death experience is symbolic of death or a catastrophic end to certain aspects of your life.

Near-death experiences are serious events. As I mentioned before, our ancestors want us to be well and in good spirits. Thus, they allow such encounters to wake us up to the reality that we are going down the wrong path. So, take heed to such warnings and examine your life to determine the root cause of the experience. And make adjustments as necessary.

Chapter 5: Getting Clear Messages from Your Ancestors

Sometimes ancestral communication does not come through as clearly as we want or desire. We often have blockages in our lives that can stop or hinder us from understanding communication from our ancestors. These blockages can occur when we are spiritually deaf. Spiritual deafness is the inability to distinctly hear or receive messages from the metaphysical realm. When we don't maintain our spiritual health, we quickly lose our ability to communicate with spiritual beings. In the case of not getting clear messages from ancestors, we become spiritually deaf when we don't make a concerted effort to connect with them on a frequent basis.

They still communicate with us even when we don't connect with them. And yes, we do receive some messages from them even if we are not intentionally or consistently connecting with them. However, when we are in this state, ancestral messages can often be confusing or incomprehensible. In which case, we typically ignore their subtle cues since we are not aware of or used to their voice.

This same phenomenon occurs when you start interacting with someone who speaks with a distinctly different accent than your own. You may catch a few words here and there. But it will be difficult for you to have a clear or deep understanding of what the person is saying if you don't spend time getting used to their way of speaking.

The same is true in regards to communicating with your ancestors. The more time you spend with them, the more you are able to understand their mode of communication. Deliberately connecting with your ancestors enhances dialogue with them on many levels as it helps you easily discern their voice. It also allows you to gain a better understanding of the messages that they are trying to convey.

But don't be discouraged if you have challenges deciphering ancestral communication - spiritual deafness is not a permanent condition. Once you implement the proper tools, you can quickly overcome this issue. You can do many things to enhance the flow of communication between you and your ancestors. These methods will ultimately help you establish more robust and consistent interaction. The more you implement the techniques - the better. You can apply as many methods as you choose. The key is to consistently use the tools that are most effective for you.

Energy Clearing

There are several methods available for clearing negative or stagnant energy from your environment.

The first rule of thumb is to maintain a clean space. Cluttered and dirty environments attract malevolent or evil spirits. Therefore, the first thing you need to do before engaging in energy clearing work is to thoroughly clean your space.

Once you have cleaned your space, you can wipe down hard surfaces with a spiritual cologne such as Florida water, rose water, sage spray, etc. You can also spray spiritual colognes in the air. Likewise, you can smudge the space with energy-clearing incense, herbs, and resins like sage, palo santo, or cedarwood.

As you clear the energy, speak to it and command it to leave your space. Inform the spirit that it is not welcomed or wanted in your environment. And let it know that it must leave. Your words have power, and lower-level energies must submit to it. These types of spirits are more afraid of us than we are of them.

Frequency of Veneration

As mentioned several times, the more you engage in ancestor veneration, the better the results. As with anything, you get out of it what you put into it. You should always follow your intuition and do what works best for you. There is no set amount of time or specific days required for ancestral veneration unless you practice within a spiritual system that indicates such. However, a frequent and consistent practice enhances communication channels.

I commune with my ancestors every day, and I engage in ritual work dedicated to my ancestors once a week. I also steadily maintain many of the other practices previously outlined. There are times when I miss my regular schedule for these activities, but my routine is relatively consistent otherwise. Through my diligent efforts, I have received many powerful and beneficial messages from my ancestors.

As mentioned, the more time you spend with a person, the better you can understand their communication style. You begin to recognize their voice immediately. After spending a prolonged time with them, you can even predict what they will say or how they will react in certain situations. The same is true when it comes to spending quality time with your ancestors. You will begin to recognize when they are speaking to you. You will know their response before they even give it.

Conversely, if you spend scarce time with them, it will be challenging to recognize when they speak to you. You may not notice the subtle clues that they give or the soft whispers that they utter. Thus, if you want to strengthen your communication with your ancestors, spend more time with them. You can implement many of the techniques mentioned in the chapter about connecting with your ancestors. You can likewise use other tools that work best for you.

Nutrition and Exercise

While the two may seem unrelated, eating healthy and exercising are essential elements for receiving clear communication from your ancestors. Consuming nutritious, wholesome meals contribute to clear thinking, a peaceful mood, and positive thoughts. Good health plays a vital role in our ability to effectively commune with the spirit world.

When we are at our mental, emotional, and physical best, we attract good and benevolent spirits into our space. We can likewise better discern their voice when our mind is clear and free of ruminations and other distracting thoughts. A healthy lifestyle inclusive of nutritious foods and regular physical activity is key to maintaining optimal mental, emotional, and physical performance.

Conversely, the buildup of toxins and poisons in our bodies can lead to sluggish, cloudy thinking, negative thoughts, unpleasant mood swings, etc. This buildup is often caused by poor dietary habits and a sedentary lifestyle. Such an environment is a breeding ground for unwelcome and unwanted spiritual contact. It likewise disrupts the flow of positive, beneficial communication from our ancestors and other benevolent spirits. Therefore, if you wish to enhance your communication with your ancestors, you should engage in healthier lifestyle habits.

Likewise, you should avoid or limit the consumption of toxic substances such as alcohol, smoke, sugar, caffeine, etc. You can have some of these vices in moderation. However, you need to engage in healthy behaviors more often to combat any adverse effects from such toxic substances. Also, you should always avoid engaging in ancestor veneration practices whenever you consume certain toxins.

For instance, it is never a good idea to go to your ancestor altar intoxicated from alcohol, illicit substances, and certain pharmaceuticals. If you do, you will make yourself a target for demonic spirits that will try to usurp your energy and ultimately use you for evil purposes. This aspect of spiritual communication is discussed in more detail in a later chapter.

Fasting

Fasting is an age-old spiritual practice that has been used for centuries by many religious adherents of different belief systems throughout the world. However, it is not specific to any religious or spiritual system - it can be a beneficial tool for anyone.

Religious or spiritual fasts typically involve abstaining from food and water or only food for a prescribed amount of time. Some people only abstain from certain foods like animal flesh, bread, or dairy during a fast. Usually, spiritual fasts are combined with prayer and spending time in solitude. Many people also abstain from other vices and distractions such as alcohol, smoking, social media, etc., during periods of fasting.

Fasts are beneficial for many reasons. When done correctly and consistently, they are excellent for cleaning the spiritual and physical body. Fasting can remove blockages that are keeping you from engaging in clear spiritual communication. They can likewise be instrumental in healing some physical conditions. Such benefits of fasting are usually experienced during longer fasts or shorter, more frequent fasting periods. However, there is no set amount of time recommended for conducting a fast. Though, careful consideration should be given to any health conditions that might be exacerbated or otherwise adversely affected by fasting.

When conducted with the right intentions and properly executed, fasts can be incredibly beneficial in opening the lines of communication between you and your ancestors. As stated, abstaining from all food or certain foods can clear spiritual blockages like malevolent energies that may have hindered you from connecting with your ancestors. Fasts can likewise assist with opening your third eye. In particular, prolonged fasts of 3 or more days can help your body effectively purge toxins that impede your ability to hear from Spirit.

I strongly recommend conducting weekly fasts at the beginning of your journey. Doing so will speed the process and help strengthen your connection with your ancestors. As you build your fasting muscles, longer fasting periods of 3 or more days are likewise recommended for the same purpose. Once you cleanse your spirit and body through this process, you can slow down the frequency and duration of your fasts. However, this is a tool that you can always return to whenever your connection with your ancestors feels sluggish or blocked.

Meditation

Meditation is one of the best ways to clear your mind and relax. This process helps you gain optimal focus and concentration. It is an excellent tool for opening communication channels between you and your ancestors when done with limited distractions.

Most people think about the traditional Eastern practice often performed by Hindus when they hear the word meditation. This is definitely one way to meditate. However, there are many other ways to engage in this practice. Actually, all of us have meditated at some point in time. If you are fully focused and present as you read the pages of this book, you are meditating right now.

By definition, meditation is the act of thoughtful contemplation. As a universal practice, it is not owned or co-opted by any particular cultural group. Instead, many ethnic groups have their own style and way of engaging in meditative practices. While the Hindu style can be effective, many other forms of meditation are just as beneficial. If this style appeals to you, you should make it a regular part of your routine.

However, if it challenges you, don't feel compelled to engage in it to receive clearer messages from your ancestors. Meditation should never feel forced. If you are struggling to do it, you will most likely not benefit from it. The whole point of meditating is to clear your mind, not to frustrate or overwhelm yourself.

The following list provides many effective alternative ways to meditate:

- Exercising and yoga
- Taking nature walks
- Saying affirmations
- Breathing exercises
- Getting a massage
- Singing and dancing
- Taking a spiritual bath
- Spending time in nature
- Reading inspirational books
- Visualizing or using a vision board
- Listening to high vibrational music
- Sitting in a clean, quiet environment

Each of the activities listed above provides a gateway for focused mental concentration, which is the ultimate goal of meditation. When our mind is at peace and vibrating at a high frequency, we are fully capable of communing with spirit. These activities and many others can get our minds in the ideal cognitive state for maximum focus and quietness. It is at this point that we can more effectively commune with Spirit.

Therefore, if you have challenges with ancestral communication, try to engage in a regular meditation practice. It is best to spend an hour or more in meditation every day. You can break your routine up over the course of a day and engage in several forms of meditation throughout the day. As with all things, your meditation practice should suit your personality and lifestyle. Let your intuition be your guide.

Spending Time in Nature

I have discussed this several times throughout this book, but it bears repeating in this section. Spending time in nature is an excellent way to engage in ancestor veneration. It can serve as a stand-alone mechanism for honoring your ancestors when done as part of a ritual process. However, it can likewise be a vital part of enhancing your ancestral communication. When we spend time in nature, we are among the elements. As we interact with these energies, we become refreshed, renewed, and rejuvenated.

If you live in a natural environment, you probably already receive a great deal of ancestral input. However, living in a city or urban area can impede the reception of sensory information from ancestral spirits. As such, it is vital to renew your connection with nature if you wish to strengthen your communication with your ancestors. Engaging with nature doesn't require any type of elaborate rituals or ceremonies. It also doesn't necessitate that you take an expensive vacation to some exotic destination. It is as simple as spending quality time in a natural environment such as a forest, lake, river, stream, beach, mountain, etc.

You could literally sit quietly in your backyard for 20 minutes or so to experience the bountiful gifts of nature in this regard. Other settings such as natural parks, hiking trails, or botanical gardens can make spending time in nature even more enjoyable. But again, there is no specific method required for spending quality time in nature. The goal is to simply get out and be among the elements on a regular basis. Ultimately, you need to recharge your batteries so that you can empower your connection with your ancestors.

Sun Gazing

The ancient practice of sungazing is thought to be very effective for opening the pineal gland. The pineal gland is considered to be our third or spiritual eye. It's the space where we receive intuitive messages from the spiritual realm. There are many ways to "open" or clear this space for receiving clear messages from the spiritual realm. Many of the practices mentioned in the ancestor veneration chapter and this chapter are beneficial tools for achieving spiritual enlightenment.

Sungazing involves staring directly at the sun with the naked eye. It is theorized that the sun energizes you and gives you spiritual downloads. These downloads transfer ancient wisdom and knowledge and help us better connect with Spirit as the sunlight energy. You can typically receive highly evolved messages through sungazing if you continuously engage in this practice.

Many practitioners of sungazing agree that the best time to sun gaze is within one hour after sunrise and one hour before sunset. During these intervals, the sun is less intense and easier to look at, especially for beginners. However, I know people who sun gaze at other times, such as midday. But I only recommend this option for advanced sun gazers.

Sungazing should be performed with the naked eye. You should not stare at the sun through a window, lenses (sunglasses, eyeglasses, contacts, etc.), or other shielding devices. Otherwise, it will not have the same beneficial effects. It is typically recommended that beginners start sun gazing for about 10-30 second intervals at sunrise or sunset. Thereafter, you can increase your sessions by 10 seconds each day and ultimately work your way up to 30 minutes or more per session.

In addition to enhancing your spiritual connection, sun gazing is thought to have the following effects:

- Improvement in eyesight and visual acuity
- Improvement in emotional and mental health
- Alleviation or elimination of physical disease states
- Decreased hunger sensations or need for physical nourishment
- Increased production of serotonin and melatonin

Crystals and Stones

The use of crystals and stones takes advantage of the earth element, which can be extremely helpful for grounding or stabilizing ancestral connections. Natural crystals and stones found in various locations throughout the earth are said to have multiple healing properties.

Crystals and stones reportedly have the power to transmute negative energy and enhance the flow of positive energy. Though there isn't much scientific evidence to back such claims, many people swear by the healing and transformative powers of these natural elements. Crystals and stones are thought to aid in clearing spaces of unclean energies, enhancing meditative practices, and connecting with the spirit realm.

Some of the most potent crystals known explicitly for connecting with the ancestral realm include jade, turquoise, and malachite. Other crystals and stones commonly used for connecting with the spiritual realm in general include:

- Amethyst
- Labradorite
- Celestite
- Lapis Lazuli
- Clear Quartz
- Smoky Quartz
- Hematite
- Green Aventurine
- Amazonite

Many other crystals also enhance spiritual communication and contact. These elements work differently for each individual. The key is to find what resonates with you and work with that energy accordingly. Some people select crystals and stones based solely on what "speaks to them." Conversely, some people research crystals and stones based on their meaning or spiritual properties and then make their selections. Either approach can be beneficial when using your intuition as a guide.

You can use crystals and stones in many ways to enhance your connection with your ancestors. You can wear them in the form of jewelry, place them on your ancestor altar, use them during meditation sessions, etc. Since they are earth elements, they are very effective for balancing our connection with Spirit and helping us maintain a strong foundation in the earthly realm.

Summary

This chapter included many tools and resources that you can use to enhance your communication with your ancestors. You can use some or all of the suggestions outlined in this chapter. For best results, I recommend trying whatever feels right to you. But, try to implement them one at a time so that you can better assess the impact of whatever methods you choose.

Take your time to become familiar with the tools you select. Also, implement each method based on your personality and style. If it doesn't work for you, don't be afraid to let it go and try something else. You may find that you work with one method for some time, stop for a while, and then come back to it later. The method may become one of your favorite means of enhancing communication with your ancestors after establishing a consistent rhythm.

Developing a sound and effective ancestral veneration practice is a process. It requires trial and error to figure out what works best for you. Rarely does it automatically flow for the average person. Even advanced practitioners have questions, doubts, and stagnation in ancestral communication at times. In addition to developing a connection with our ancestors, we have to deal with everyday life, which can easily get us off track. So be gentle and patient with yourself as you embark on this journey.

Chapter 6: Reconciling Broken Ancestral Ties

While it is a beautiful blessing for our ancestors to take care of us from the astral realm, sometimes these benefits are hindered by situations beyond our control. Such interferences usually occur when we have broken ancestral ties that need to be repaired. Our ancestors can and do work on our behalf even when our connection with them is broken or disrupted. However, there are certain things that they can't do when there are significant breaks or tears in our ancestral lineage.

If your living family doesn't engage in ancestral veneration, this is an indicator that your ancestral ties need to be repaired. Likewise, if your family suffers from persistent adverse generational patterns such as drug and alcohol abuse, sexual abuse, domestic violence, imprisonment, etc., this is a sign of broken ancestral connections. These patterns may not directly affect you, but if they impact a disproportionate number of your family members, your family may be suffering from a generational curse.

Sadly, many people throughout the African diaspora are enduring immeasurable suffering for this very reason. Many of our ancestors were forced to stop practicing their traditions and subsequently compelled to adopt the religion of their captors. We lost a great deal of ancestral wisdom and knowledge through this process, which has caused a critical chasm in many families and societies throughout the African diaspora. Honestly, the only way to remedy this situation is by reconciling our broken ancestral ties. And, this can take some serious time, effort, and energy depending on the nature of the problem in each family line. But don't get discouraged - it is well worth the time and effort to see your family made whole again.

My Ancestral Reconciliation Experience

If you read my biography at the beginning of this book, you know by now that I practice Haitian Vodou and Ifa. While I have both Haitian and Yoruba heritage, I was born in America, and all of my known relatives from as far back as slavery times were born in America. I imagine this to be the case for most African Americans living in the south. Many of us have family ties with the people groups in the Caribbean Islands, and South and Central America.

But in my case, I was born and raised as an African American though I knew about my indigenous-American roots from an early age. However, when I was growing up, I knew nothing about my African or Haitian heritage. Like most African Americans (AAs), I knew that all AAs had an ancestral connection to Africa through the Transatlantic slave trade process. But that was it. My immediate family never discussed our African heritage, and they certainly were not into Pan-Africanism, Black nationalism, or the like.

There was a brief moment during my childhood when my paternal grandmother and step-father got some dashikis made in the early '90s during one of the many revivals of the black conscious movement. This happened during the era when Queen Latifah was singing about unity, and all the hip-hop stars were rapping about black nationalism and wearing dashikis. But even then, there was no significant discussion of our heritage or what it meant for them to wear this type of garb. It was just a brief passing moment that served as a glimpse to my introduction into Black and African consciousness.

It wasn't until I was in my late 30's that I started to truly learn about the history of black people and our traditional spiritual systems. Throughout my childhood and through my late 20's, I was a typical Bible-believing Christian. As I was transitioning into my 30's, I started learning about the Hebrew Israelite belief system. After some time, I became heavily involved in these teachings.

I studied the teachings of this doctrine for about 6-7 years before I ventured into African spirituality. The Hebrew Israelite faith served as my gateway into the two systems that I currently practice. While I no longer fully subscribe to the teachings of the Hebrew Israelite belief system, I do believe in some of their teachings.

As I continued to study African spirituality, I experienced another phase of my spiritual awakening. I started encountering many of the forms of ancestral communication that I mentioned earlier in this book. My ancestors began speaking to me through intuitive messages, dreams, visions, synchronicities, numbers, movies, music, nature, animals, feathers, etc. I was receiving so much feedback from them at one point that I thought that I was losing my mind. It was a wonderful yet discombobulating experience.

My ancestors taught me many things about our heritage and lineage. They showed me why I had experienced certain things in my life and that I was chosen to reconcile our broken heritage. I experienced a critical phase of my spiritual awakening journey during that time that forever reshaped my life in many ways.

About four years after this experience, I had the fortuitous opportunity to connect with a Haitian who practices Vodou from his motherland. I wasn't involved with any particular system at the time though I had studied many traditional African belief systems. After meeting him and learning that we were embarking on similar journeys, I asked him to help me get a Vodou reading. He assisted me with the process, and I ended up having about four divination sessions before I finally learned what I needed to do to reconcile my broken ancestral lineage.

Through those readings, I also learned that I had direct ancestral lineage from Haiti. This information came up in three divination sessions performed by different Manbos and Oungans (Vodou priestesses and priests). Through the Haitian system, I also learned how to engage in ancestral veneration from a traditional perspective. And I was able to break my family's generational curse through the ancestor ceremony that was prescribed during the divination sessions.

I did not discuss those specific techniques in this book because that information is best taught in a more intimate setting. Some of the processes can be a bit complicated, which makes them difficult to explain in writing. Such explanations are also tricky when someone does not have a connection to the Haitian Vodou system. The veneration practices outlined in this book are general guidelines that anyone can effectively implement, regardless of their religious or spiritual background.

If you wish to learn practices related to a specific system, it is best to connect with a person or group fully versed in it. However, be very careful when opening spiritual portals, especially through sacred rites and ritual ceremonies. I don't recommend doing it without the guidance of a trained and qualified individual. Otherwise, you can make some costly or detrimental mistakes.

Divination Tools and Techniques

There are plenty of divination tools and techniques that can assist you in ancestral reconciliation. As mentioned, I also practice Ifa, which can be an effective divination tool for uncovering and reconciling broken familiar ties. However, I usually refer my clients to ancestral-based spiritual systems for this type of divination work. In my experience, Orisha communication has been more prominent in my Ifa readings.

Additionally, I recommend that people start with an ancestral-based spiritual system if they are interested in ancestral veneration or African spirituality in general. I especially recommend this type of advancement through traditional spirituality for African diasporans who have been disconnected from their heritage for several generations. When we first encounter a traditional system, many of us lack the necessary ancestral ties and wisdom to adequately engage with Orishas, Loas, primordial energies, etc.

Aside from Haitian Vodou, many ancestral-based systems can be effective for this purpose. The following list outlines common ancestor-based systems practiced throughout the diaspora. These systems are not listed in any particular order or hierarchy. Aside from Hoodoo, I have no personal or familiar associations with any of them. Therefore, I implore you to research before choosing either of these systems. It is vital to make an informed decision in relation to your spirituality.

The following ancestral-based systems are some practices derived from traditional African spiritual systems that may enhance your ancestral veneration practice. However, note that this list is not all-inclusive. Other systems may appeal to you as well.

- Hoodoo
- Lucumi
- Santeria
- Obeah
- Candomblé
- Umbanda
- Macumba
- Quimbanda
- 21 Divisions
- Espiritismo
- Trinidad Orisha
- Gullah-Geechee
- Louisiana Voodoo

Ancestral Communication

If you don't feel comfortable or don't know which direction to go in regarding divination, you can also consult with your ancestors. You should ask them how to reconcile broken ancestral ties even if you plan to use divination. They can lead you to the right system and the right diviner for this purpose.

Chapter 7: Discerning Spiritual Communication

As I mentioned several times, many types of spirits can and do communicate with us on a consistent basis. These spirits often use many of the same communication tactics as ancestral spirits. Your Ori (Higher Self) can speak to you via audible messages. Your Egbe (heavenly/soul mates) can hide things from you or cause you to be ill to get your attention. Orishas, Loas, and other primordial energies can show up in your dreams and affect various changes in your life. Inevitably, any spirit can connect with you using multiple forms of communication. This includes both benevolent and malevolent spirits.

So how can you discern the difference between ancestral spirits and other types of spirits? Or benevolent and malevolent spirits?

It will probably be difficult for the average beginner, who may not have as much knowledge about the hierarchy of spiritual beings. It can even be challenging at times for a more advanced practitioner in certain circumstances. In general, if you are receiving messages that inform or enlighten you, it usually doesn't make much of a difference who is delivering the information. In such instances, the spirit only serves as a messenger, whereas the message is the essential element of the communication.

Conversely, when a spirit tries to get your attention for a specific purpose, it may be detrimental for you to know which spirit is communicating with you. It could be that you need to perform a particular ritual or complete a certain task directly related to a specific energy. In which case, knowing which spirit to appease is vital.

Regardless of which spirit is communicating with you, a strong connection with your ancestors is essential. As I have mentioned several times, your ancestors are your first line of defense in spiritual matters. They advocate on your behalf just as our living relatives (parents, guardians, etc.) do in the physical realm. If you have an established relationship with your ancestors, they will lead you in the right direction in regards to determining the source of spiritual communication when necessary.

There are several other ways to determine which spirit is communicating with you. The first method is through the spirit itself. Ancestral and other spirits sometimes reveal themselves in dreams or other forms of communication. In which case, you will undoubtedly know the source. You may see specific ancestors in your dreams or smell scents associated with a particular ancestor. Or you may even intuitively know which spirit is speaking to you.

If you don't receive these types of direct cues, you can ask which spirits are communicating with you. If you need to know this information, it will be revealed to you. You may get an answer right away, or it could take days, months, or years. You will know when you need to know.

Therefore, I recommend maintaining a journal of these types of encounters. Write the date, the message you received, and any other pertinent information about the spiritual encounter in a journal - leave some space after the entry to record whatever information you receive thereafter. Additional relevant information may include the time, place, or circumstances surrounding when you received the message. If you experienced synchronicities during the delivery of the message, this information might also be instrumental.

Whenever you receive the answer to your inquiry, likewise record it and the date of receipt in the journal. Include this information in the blank space after the original entry. This process will better help you understand spiritual communication patterns.

As mentioned, sometimes it is critical to understand which spirit is sending you a message. It may be necessary for you to appease or work with a specific energy to overcome a challenge such as an illness, domestic problem, financial hardship, or similar concerns. In such instances, it may be necessary to seek out divination. Divination services provided by an experienced and skilled spiritualist can provide you with vital information about the source and intent of the message. The divination tools and techniques discussed in the previous chapter can help you determine the best route to take when selecting a diviner.

Another method is to tease out the essence or vibe of the energy. This process can help you decipher between clean and unclean spirits. Clean energies inspire, motivate, and uplift us. If you feel energized or alert after a spiritual encounter, a benevolent energy is most likely coming to bring you good tidings. Good spirits can also send us warning messages to help us be cautious. While we may feel uneasy or wary when receiving such messages, our entire vibe or mood won't entirely be affected when dealing with benevolent spirits.

Conversely, if you experience unwarranted anxiety, fear, nervousness, depression, etc., evil spirits are probably connecting with you. These types of spirits invoke negative and unproductive emotions and feelings within us. Their entire objective is to keep us operating in low vibrational energy. They are not here for our benefit, which means that we should make every effort to expel such energies from our environment whenever they are present. I discuss how to do this in the next chapter.

Chapter 8: Dealing with Unwelcome Spirits

Any time you open a spiritual portal, you present an opportunity for malevolent and other unwelcome spirits to come in. Earthbound spirits, trickster spirits, and evil spirits can enter through spiritual portals in the same way as benevolent spirits. This is not something to be fearful of, nor should it stop you from venerating your ancestors. Understand that these types of energies will come around no matter what we do. Thankfully, ancestral veneration actually assists with protecting us from these energies.

Even so, whenever you connect with the spiritual realm, there is a possibility of inviting unwanted spirits into your space. Likewise, unwanted energies can enter your environment through other people, places, and things. As such, it is best to equip yourself with the knowledge, wisdom, tools, and resources to remove unwanted energies from your environment.

The first guideline is to always protect and concentrate your space and yourself before doing spiritual work. Consecration can be performed by praying or using smudging apparatuses designed to attract benevolent spirits and dispel malevolent energies. The first thing that you should always do before starting your veneration session is to pray and invite good and benevolent ancestral spirits and spirit guides to commune with you. After that, you can command any malevolent or evil spirits to leave your space.

These types of prayers are most effective when using a smudging device such as incense or resin to purify your environment. Many types of incense and resins are adequate for smudging before engaging in spiritual work. However, frankincense and myrrh are most commonly used when interacting with ancestral spirits. Other protective incenses are also effective for this purpose. These include:

- Sage
- Copal
- Amber
- Benzoin
- Cedarwood
- Palo Santo
- Dragon's blood
- Sandalwood

The process of smudging involves sweeping the smoke of the smudging agent toward or away from your physical body or environment. You should move the smudging agent toward you in a circular motion when inviting good and benevolent energies into your space. Conversely, you should move the smudging agent away from you in a circular motion when removing or expelling negative energies.

Smudging is most effective when activated with the power of the spoken word. Therefore, as you move the smoke toward you, verbally invite clean energies into your space. Likewise, verbally expel unclean energies from your environment when guiding the smoke away from your body and physical space. As you sweep away malevolent energies, open a door or window so that they can easily dislodge from the environment.

If you are uncomfortable with speaking your prayers and commands out loud or are otherwise unable to do so, you can also say them in your mind. This method can likewise be effective, especially when you are in an environment where verbally speaking to spirits is not conducive.

Spiritual colognes such as Florida water, rose water, sage water, etc., are also effective for dispelling negative energies from a space. These types of colognes can be used on your physical body, such as your face, chin, neck, hands, feet, etc. They can also be sprayed in the air when used in a spray bottle. As with the smudging process, you want the cologne mist to move toward you when engaging with good spirits and away from you when dealing with evil entities.

How Unwanted Spirits Enter Your Space

The previously mentioned methods are protective barriers for keeping unwanted spirits at bay when engaging in spiritual communication. However, there are still circumstances when such energies can enter your space. For example, a ghost may have inhabited a particular space for a long time. It could be inside your home or in an area close to your home, such as in an alleyway. Consecration efforts may not deter this spirit. Depending on the frequency it is vibrating on, it may remain in a particular environment regardless of the foundational protective barriers that are activated. Sometimes it takes higher-level tools and techniques to remove them.

Another example is when you enter spiritual communication in a negative or agitated mood. It is much easier to attract low vibrational energies if you are angry, upset, depressed, frustrated, etc. Even if you consecrate yourself or your environment before doing spirit work, your low vibration can also negate your efforts and make the space a breeding ground for similar energies. The same is true for other people who live in your home. Their negative energy can likewise attract low-level entities. It's like leaving a door halfway open instead of fully closing it. Thus, it is best not to open spiritual portals when you are operating in low vibrational energy.

Another way these types of energies can enter your space is through a spiritual attack. Any time you engage in uplifting spiritual work, there will always be malevolent entities trying to distract and disarm you. Ultimately, that is their overriding purpose. So even if you haven't directly engaged in activities that invite negative energy into your space, they can still come to get you off track.

They often come to cause confusion, disruption, frustration, agitation, etc., in order to dissuade you from continuing your spiritual journey. These energies know that you are powerful and will be even more powerful when working with your ancestors and other benevolent spirits. They don't want you to enjoy this power, so they will attack you even when you are not actively engaging them.

Ways to Remove Unwanted Energies

But don't fret. There are ways to remove these types of entities from your space whenever they do show up. Some energies are easier to remove than others. But with diligent effort, you can rid your environment of unwanted energies that are counterproductive to your spiritual development. The remainder of this chapter outlines sound guidelines for dispelling unwelcome spirits.

You can use all or a few of them at different times. I encourage you to try each method outlined in this section to determine which one resonates with you. Many of these methods work synergistically when used in conjunction with one or more of the other methods. Keep in mind that different spirits respond to different approaches. Therefore, if one method worked at one time but did not work later, you may need to try something else.

Use Your Words

The same way you can command an unwelcome guest to leave your home, you can likewise do so with unwelcome spirits. You can literally order them to leave your space, and in most cases, they are obliged to obey you. Lower-level spiritual entities are actually under our command. They must abide by our orders, especially when we speak with unwavering authority.

If you are at a loss for words or simply feel more comfortable working with sacred texts, you can likewise use poems or passages from holy books when expelling these types of energies. The Holy Odu, Bible, Quran, Torah, etc., are sometimes helpful in this process. You do not have to be an adherent of any particular religious practice to use this method effectively.

Scriptures or passages from these sacred texts are powerful even though some of them have been altered. But this does not negate their effectiveness as spiritual weapons against evil forces. For example, many of the Psalms found in the Bible are commonly used to create a spiritual safeguard around people, places, or animals. In particular, Psalms 23, 27, and 91 have historically been used by Christians and non-Christians alike for this very purpose. As with all things, it is ultimately about intention. Any protective words that you use with conviction and authority have the power to rid certain unwanted energies from your space.

Cleanse Your Physical Body

Whenever you approach spiritual work, you should always be clean and maintain good hygiene. Toxins, dirt, debris, bad smells, etc., attract unclean energies. So, if you are not clean when you approach spiritual work, you are opening a gateway for unclean energies.

Sometimes the inside of your physical temple also needs a higher level of cleansing. If you find that you are dealing with an overwhelming number of negative emotions or burdensome thoughts, you are probably entertaining malevolent spirits. It is during this time that fasting may be in order. As I mentioned before, fasting is a great way to gain better spiritual clarity because of its ability to cleanse on a deeper level. Likewise, it is an effective way to rid your temple of toxic energies that may have taken up residence in your physical body.

Colon cleansing is another effective method for cleansing your body. If you have years of toxins built up in your system, you will need an effective way to remove these wastes. Constipation, hard stools, bloating, abdominal pain, persistent nausea, dehydration, etc., are all clues that your colon needs a deep cleansing. A colon packed with years of waste can be a breeding ground for unclean energies, as with other toxic environments. In such instances, you need to cleanse your colon to dislodge these unclean energies from your body. There are several ways to cleanse the colon, such as through enemas and colon hydrotherapy. If you have a significant buildup of toxic waste in your colon, these methods are most effective at removing them quickly. Though it may take a few sessions to get a deep level, thorough cleanse.

Herbs with laxative properties are also useful for this purpose. However, they tend to have a slower, cumulative effect. But when used in combination with other colon cleansing methods, they can work faster and be more effective. The following is a list of cleansing herbs and natural substances that are very effective for cleansing your bowel:

- Senna
- Psyllium
- Aloe vera
- Flaxseed
- Castor oil
- Magnesium
- Cascara sagrada

Cleanse Your Environment

Just as your physical body needs cleansing before engaging in spiritual work, so does your physical environment. Unclean spirits also take up residence in cluttered, dirty, smelly, pest-ridden physical spaces. At a minimum, the area that you conduct your spiritual work in needs to be clean. For instance, if you set up your ancestor altar in the corner of a room, a closet, or another small area, this space needs to be clean before you begin working in it.

It should be cleansed on a regular basis to discourage the growth or collection of dust, mold, debris, stains, bugs or insects, animal waste, etc. Trash receptacles should be emptied frequently, especially in or near a space where spiritual work is conducted. Also, trash bins in or near spiritual workspaces should be emptied when engaging in special rituals such as spiritual baths, offerings, candle rituals, etc.

These areas should also be free of clutter. Altar areas are not spaces for storing papers, clothing, or any other materials or objects. Cluttered spaces are a magnet for evil and earthbound spirits. These types of spirits like to congregate in any space where dirt, dust, waste, clutter, etc., is present. They can easily remain undetected in such areas, and they can wreak havoc in these types of environments.

Strong, pungent odors also attract unwelcome spirits. The essence of a smelly, hard-to-remove odor may indicate the presence of an evil or earthbound energy in your space. Typically, once you properly clean your environment, foul odors will go away. However, if they don't, it may be necessary to thoroughly smudge your environment.

It is also essential to maintain cleanliness in all areas of your home or other veneration space. Your home or spiritual workspace doesn't have to be spotless but should maintain a modicum of cleanliness at all times. Doing so attracts good and benevolent energies while simultaneously repelling evil or malevolent spirits. So, if you find that your smudging or other protective efforts are not working take a look at your physical environment to determine if it needs sprucing up.

Use Salt, Crystals, and Stones

I have mentioned each of these tools in other sections of this book. They are all excellent spiritual tools that can be maintained on an ancestral altar. Doing so consistently will keep evil energies away from your sacred space. However, as mentioned previously, sometimes evil spirits are still granted an entryway through various mechanisms.

Salt is a potent antidote for dispelling evil spirits. If you are dealing with a particularly stubborn energy, you can throw salt in every corner of your dwelling to chase it from your space. You can also throw salt in the corner of entryways to your home to keep evil energies from entering with guests or others who may come to your home. Salt is likewise good to put in spiritual baths or for cleansing spiritual items.

Similar to salt, crystals and stones are earth-based elements useful for dispelling evil energies and protecting a sacred space. Several crystals and stones are helpful for this purpose. It is usually beneficial to place these elements in your sacred space and on your body for extra protection.

Use Noisemakers and High Pitch Frequencies

Bells, cymbals, gongs, spiritual rattles, rhythmic chanting, drums, other noisemakers, and high-pitched frequencies can also shake out unclean spirits. Such devices are powerful tools for waking up positive energies and repelling negative energies. This is the very reason why bells, whistles, tambourines, horns, pom poms, clappers, and similar devices are used to rouse team spirit at sporting events. They are employed to shake up a winning, victorious spirit while discouraging the spirit of defeat and failure.

This is also the exact reason why gospel songs are often expressed in high-pitched frequencies along with shouting or screaming. Our ancestors were well aware of the power of such tones in the process of praise and worship. Using such techniques was one of the few tools that many had access to during the Transatlantic slavery period of the Americas. And we continue to use this powerful and effective dispeller of evil spirits in the African American church today. Though, many are probably not aware of its significance.

When used in this manner, the purpose of noisemaking devices is to invite good and benevolent spirits into a space. These spirits are often instrumental in assisting with the removal of evil and unwanted energies. Likewise, the noisemaker itself distracts evil spirits because they are uncomfortable around high-pitched sounds. Therefore, the use of noisemakers amplifies the power of ridding a space of evil energies two-fold.

Before slavery, our ancestors used drums and dance for this same purpose. In fact, this method is still used in many parts of Africa today within spiritual communities. The drum also has the power to invoke a trance state and allow the entrance of a spirit into a living vessel such as a human.

Thus, if you are struggling with negative energy within yourself or your environment, use some type of noisemaker to stir the spirit. This method is a great way to set the mood or tone before spiritual work. Any of the devices mentioned in this section are useful for these purposes. You can engage the tool yourself or play pre-recorded sounds of drums, bells, whistles, etc. It is fairly easy to find African drumming beats, Asian bell and bowl sounds, Shamanic rattle music, etc., on the internet.

You can even sing or play high-pitched gospel music to achieve the same goal. Remember, you don't have to practice Christianity to use the spiritual techniques propitiated through this system. As mentioned, many of the tools used in this religion were derived from traditional African spiritual systems. So, it is not necessary to submit to the beliefs of a particular belief system to benefit from the tools and resources that our ancestors developed through it.

Work with a Spiritualist

I have mentioned this option a few times throughout this book. If you are dealing with spiritual phenomena that you cannot control or do not know how to control, reach out to a spiritualist. It is not in your best interest to allow malevolent or other non-beneficial spirits to remain in your environment. You should expel them as efficiently and quickly as possible.

However, be sure to reach out to someone who has experience working with spirits in this way. Astrologers and physics are generally unable to clear negative energies in the same way as traditional healers or Shamans. Shamans are individuals trained to work directly with spirits and have the ability to remove unwanted energies.

Shamans go by many names such as Manbos, Oungans, Babalawos, Iyanifas, sangomas, witchdoctors, etc. So don't allow the title "shaman" to hinder you from seeking out someone from your traditional belief system. The key is to find the right person to assist you. It may take some time, so be patient. Every spiritualist is not adept at working with all types of spirits.

While I advocate working with spiritual healers, diviners, mentors, etc., in many respects, I strongly encourage you to make this a last resort when removing unwanted spirits. Though these individuals are usually highly trained in this function, everyone has the capacity and authority to work with spirits on some level.

It is essential that you exercise this ability yourself and not be wholly dependent on someone else for this type of spiritual work all the time. Otherwise, you will consistently lean on others for a function that you should be dealing with yourself (if you are capable of doing so).

Chapter 9: Conclusion

Ancestor veneration is an effective yet highly intuitive process. There is no "right" way to do it. Though there are foundational principles involved in the practice, people from different traditions and backgrounds often have varying experiences with ancestor veneration. While they may not all use the same methods or techniques, many people have enjoyable and successful experiences when venerating their ancestors.

The purpose of this book is not to provide a template for ancestral veneration. Instead, it is designed to give you safe, sound, and responsible ideas and advice for cultivating your practice. All of the tools, techniques, and resources outlined in this book are tried and true. They have worked for me, my clients, and many others.

I have personally used the majority of the ancestor veneration methods and experienced most of the forms of ancestor communication outlined in this book. Additionally, I know individuals who have used or encountered the methods and mechanisms that I haven't. That's how I know that they work. While other tools may be just as effective for ancestral veneration, I did not include some of them because I do not have direct experience working with them. Also, other methods that I use are specific to the traditions that I practice within and are best taught in more intimate settings. So, keep an open mind as you explore this topic in more depth.

Ancestor veneration is ultimately about intention. If you engage in this practice to develop a closer connection to your lost loved ones so that you can fulfill your destiny, you are on the right track. In doing so, your ancestors will guide you to the right tools, resources, and mentors for developing your practice.

Contrarily, if your goal is only to petition your ancestors for material things, your intentions are not pure. The same holds true if you don't plan to give anything to your ancestors for their assistance. The goal of connecting to your ancestors is to develop a relationship. Only approaching them for their help and never giving anything in return will not lead to a balanced, harmonized relationship. As such, you will most likely not be successful or satisfied with the results of your practice.

As you continue to honor your ancestors, you may find that the tools and techniques you use change over time. And that's perfectly normal. As I stated several times throughout this book, there are many ways to engage in ancestral veneration. It is perfectly fine to alter or modify your practice to suit your personal needs. Your process is meant to grow with you.

In general, spiritual work is subjective. It's the inner sense of knowing that shows you when you are on the right path. Thus, you need to stay deeply connected to your inner self. In doing so, you will easily find the best approach for your ancestral veneration practice. If something doesn't feel authentic to you, don't do it. You will most likely not enjoy or effectively execute methods that are not meant for you. But if something does resonate with you, explore it in more depth, make it your own, and trust the process.

Made in the USA
Middletown, DE
09 March 2023

26482094R00096